HUMAN MOVEMENT

How the Body Walks, Runs, Jumps, and Kicks

INQUIRE AND INVESTIGATE

Carla Mooney
Illustrated by Sam Carbaugh

Nomad Press
A division of Nomad Communications
10 9 8 7 6 5 4 3 2 1

This book was manufactured by Marquis Book Printing,
Montmagny, Québec, Canada
March 2017, Job #134264
ISBN Softcover: 978-1-61930-485-7
ISBN Hardcover: 978-1-61930-481-9

Educational Consultant, Marla Conn

Questions regarding the ordering of this book should be addressed to
Nomad Press
2456 Christian St.
White River Junction, VT 05001
www.nomadpress.net

Printed in Canada.

Recent science titles in the
Inquire and Investigate series

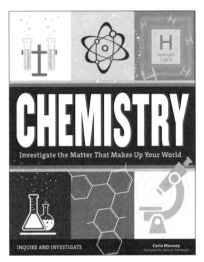

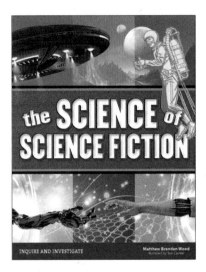

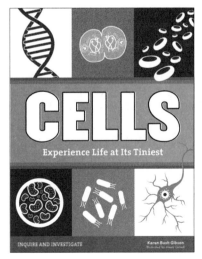

Interested in primary sources?

PS

Look for this icon.

You can use a smartphone or tablet app to scan the QR codes and explore more! Cover up neighboring QR codes to make sure you're scanning the right one. You can find a list of URLs on the Resources page.

If the QR code doesn't work, try searching the Internet with the Keyword Prompts to find other helpful sources.

🔎 Human Movement

Contents

Timeline vi

Introduction
Forces and Motion in the Human Body 1

Chapter 1
The Skeleton 11

Chapter 2
The Muscular System 25

Chapter 3
The Brain-Body Connection 43

Chapter 4
Help From the Organs 59

Chapter 5
Fuel to Move 77

Chapter 6
Moving On 93

Glossary ▾ Metric Conversions ▾ Resources ▾ Index

TIMELINE

776 BCE .... Some of the first athletic competitions take place at Olympia in Greece as part of religious festivals held to honor the Greek gods.

400s BCE .... The Greek physician Herodicus is the first Western physician to combine sports and exercise with medicine and is considered to be the father of sports medicine.

460–375 BCE ...... Ancient Greek physician Hippocrates emphasizes the health benefits of diet, exercise, and overall fitness. He prescribes gymnastics and exercise to strengthen and build up the body against disease.

384–322 BCE ...... Ancient Greek philosopher and scientist Aristotle is the first person to study and describe general body movements and the forces needed for movement. He becomes known as the "Father of Kinesiology."

287–212 BCE ...... Archimedes, an ancient Greek mathematician, physicist, engineer, inventor, and astronomer, discovers many basic laws of physics that are integral to understanding and describing human movement. These include laws governing levers and buoyancy.

129–c. 216 CE ..... Ancient Roman physician Galen observes that there are two types of blood—dark in the veins and bright in the arteries. He also identifies two different nerve pathways in the body—the sensory path for receiving information and the motor path for sending messages to the muscles.

1452–1519.......... Italian painter and inventor Leonardo da Vinci creates detailed illustrations of the human body, including drawings of the muscles, tendons, ligaments, and bones.

1628................... English physician William Harvey describes in detail the circulation and properties of blood through the body and heart.

1638................... Italian astronomer, physicist, and mathematician Galileo Galilei publishes a book about his life's work on the science of motion and the strength of materials.

1687................... Isaac Newton publishes his book, *Mathematical Principles of Natural Philosophy*, which includes his three laws of physics that govern movement. These laws form the basis of biomechanics.

1786................... Scientist Luigi Galvani observes a muscle contraction when a frog's leg is touched with a metallic rod charged with static electricity. He conducts further experiments to confirm that electrical stimulation triggers muscle contraction.

1890................... French scientist Étienne-Jules Marey records the electrical activity during a muscle contraction and introduces the term "electromyography," the recording of electrical activity of muscle tissue.

1904–1905.......... American physical education instructor Luther Halsey Gulick organizes the Academy of Physical Education to bring together those who are doing original scientific work in physical training and to promote their work.

1926................... The American Academy of Kinesiology and Physical Education is founded to encourage and promote the study and educational applications of the art and science of human movement and physical activity. It is now known as the National Academy of Kinesiology.

1970–1980.......... Brain scanning is developed, giving scientists a new window into the brain and how it controls movement.

1990................... Scientists develop functional magnetic resonance imaging (fMRI) to study the brain as it works to control movement.

2015................... Scientists discover unique muscle fibers in the upper airway in humans that might be linked to snoring and sleep apnea.

2016................... An international team of scientists use a wireless "brain-spinal interface" to bypass spinal cord injuries in a pair of rhesus monkeys, restoring intentional walking movement to a temporarily paralyzed leg.

Forces and Motion in the Human Body

How does your body move and how does that affect your health?

Different forces act on your body's systems to create different types of movement.

The human body was made for movement. Every day, you move different parts of your body, from your head to your toes. All bodies move differently. Even picking up this book and turning the pages involves moving your body. Have you ever wondered how your body moves?

How does your arm know where to reach and catch a ball? When you play the piano, how do your fingers know which keys to strike? How does your body adjust to a new workout routine? The answers to these questions can all be found in the study of human movement.

Moving an arm or a leg might seem like a simple task. But human movement is actually very complex. Movement is a change in place, position, or posture in relation to the environment. Movement happens only when different body systems, such as the skeletal system, cardiovascular system, neuromuscular system, and the body's energy systems, work together. To move successfully, these systems interact and adapt to a constantly changing environment.

> Kinesiology is the science of human movement.

Kinesiology studies how the body initiates and controls movement, beginning with the brain and using all the different body systems. It studies the body at rest and in motion and examines how body systems interact during different types of movement.

Kinesiology also studies how the body adapts and changes as a result of motion. Using this knowledge, kinesiology professionals are able to improve the body's performance, help people avoid injury, and improve physical fitness. Kinetics is the study of the impact that different forces have on mechanical systems, such as your body.

FORCES AND MOTION

As you move throughout your day, forces act on your body. When you walk down the street, twirl on the dance floor, or even just sit in a chair, invisible forces affect your body and its movement. A force is a push or pull on an object that results from the object's interaction with another object. When two objects interact, there is a force acting on each of them. When the interaction ends, the objects no longer experience that force.

Objects move when forces are applied to them. English scientist Isaac Newton explained the way that motion works in his three laws of motion.

MOTI N TION

The term *kinesiology* comes from the Greek word *kine*, meaning "to move," and *ology*, meaning "the study of." It's a word to describe the mechanics and structure of the body in relation to movement.

VOCAB LAB

There is a lot of new vocabulary in this book! Turn to the glossary in the back when you come to a word you don't understand. Practice your new vocabulary in the **VOCAB LAB** activities in each chapter.

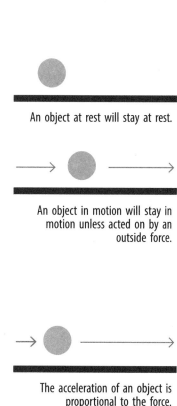

An object at rest will stay at rest.

An object in motion will stay in motion unless acted on by an outside force.

The acceleration of an object is proportional to the force.

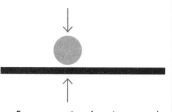

As the mass increases, the acceleration decreases.

For every action there is an equal and opposite reaction.

Newton's three laws of motion define all types of motion, including the movement of your body.

- **Law of inertia:** An object at rest will stay at rest and an object in motion will stay in constant linear motion unless acted on by an outside force. If a ball is rolling, it will keep rolling forever unless something stops it. In the same way, if a ball is at rest, it will stay at rest until a force pushes it to move.

- **Law of acceleration:** The acceleration of an object is directly proportional to the force acting on it and inversely proportional to the mass of the object. As the force acting upon an object increases, the acceleration of the object also increases. As the mass of an object increases, the acceleration of the object decreases for a fixed force.

- **Law of action and reaction:** For every action there is an equal and opposite reaction. When one object exerts a force on a second object, the second object reacts by exerting an equal force in the opposite direction on the first object. For example, when you walk, your body pushes down on the ground to move yourself forward. The ground pushes back against you with the same magnitude of force, propelling you forward.

The movement of the human body follows Newton's laws of motion. The body moves when internal and external forces act on it. Internal forces are generated within the body. When a muscle contracts, it applies an internal pulling force on a bone, which causes movement. External forces are generated outside of the body. For example, when you fall, the force of gravity pulls you down.

FORCES AND MECHANICAL LOADS

Every second of the day, different forces act on your body. They affect the body and its structures at rest and during movement. The effects of these forces on the body are called mechanical loads.

For example, a compression load occurs when a force pushes or squeezes on an object. Did you know that you are taller at the beginning of the day than you are at the end of the day? During the day, the force of gravity and your body weight create a compression load that squeezes your spine and bones, pushing them closer together and making you shrink. At night, the compression load is lifted when you're lying down asleep, letting your spine and bones stretch back out.

Other mechanical loads that affect the body include tension, bending, torsion, and shear loads. Tension occurs when a force pulls on an object. When your muscles pull on your bones, they apply tension. Bending occurs when the forces of tension and compression occur together. When a compression force acts on one side of an object and a tension force acts on the other side, the object bends.

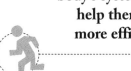
MOTION NOTION

Torsion occurs when one end of an object is fixed and the object twists around an axis. When a playing field has a lot of friction, it can cause an athlete's foot to become fixed on the ground. Twisting forces on the knee or ankle can cause torsion and lead to injury.

[Have you ever broken a bone? It may have been caused by a shear load on the bone.]

Shear forces push one part of the body one way, while simultaneously pushing another part of the body in the opposite direction. A shear force can displace a part of an object. For example, if a shear force hits your shin bone while your ankle is fixed firmly on the ground, one portion of the shin may be displaced, causing the bone to break.

During many activities, the human body experiences several types of forces and loads simultaneously. Combined loads occur when more than one type of load is delivered to an object.

FORMS OF MOTION

Biomechanists often divide movement into three categories—linear, angular, and general.

Linear motion occurs when all parts of an object move in the same direction. The object can move in a straight line, called rectilinear motion. A passenger in a car going down a straight road is an example of rectilinear motion.

A type of linear motion called curvilinear motion moves in an arc. A child who stays upright on a swing demonstrates curvilinear motion.

Angular motion occurs when an object rotates about an axis. An ice skater performing a spin is an example of angular motion. Many of the motions your body makes are angular motions. For example, when your muscles contract and pull a bone, they cause the bone to rotate above a joint.

General motion occurs when linear motion and angular motions combine. Human movements are almost always examples of general motion. When you walk, your joints are rotating in angular motion, but your entire body is moving in a straight line, in linear motion.

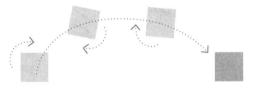

FOUNDATIONS OF MOVEMENT

To move, the human body goes through a complex series of interactions that involve different body systems. Even the very tiniest movement requires coordination. Communication between the muscular, skeletal, and nervous systems all come into play.

- **Skeletal system:** The human skeleton is the framework that supports the human body. Without bones, you could not stand, sit, or walk.

- **Muscular system:** Muscles are connected to bones. When a muscle contracts, it often produces movement around a joint. Sometimes, muscle contraction does not produce movement, but instead supports the body and increases stability.

- **Nervous system:** Every movement you make is controlled by the nervous system, or brain-body connection. The brain interprets signals from the body and sends messages to the muscles to move. These messages travel through the nerves of the nervous system until they reach their destinations.

You can think of your body as an ecosystem with lots of different parts that work both independently and with all the other parts to keep the whole body healthy.

While each of these systems is important on its own, by working together they create movement. For example, think about something as simple as walking across a room. When you first decide to walk, your brain determines your body position, evaluates where you are, and sends a message to certain muscles to move. When activated, the muscles contract and move your body across the floor. While some muscles are active, others are preparing for action. Throughout the process, your skeletal system holds it all together, supporting your body so that you can stand and walk.

MOVEMENT FOR HEALTH

What's the big deal about moving your body? Movement is important because the human body is most efficient when it is used regularly. When a person stays at rest for too long, the body begins to weaken. Without regular use, muscles lose mass. That means you should exercise and use your body as much as you are able so your muscles stay healthy.

In addition, being inactive causes a decline in bone density, making your bones weaker and more likely to break. Inactivity can even cause your heart size to decrease, making it harder for it to pump blood throughout your body.

Lack of movement sometimes leads to unhealthy weight gain. According to the National Institutes of Health, more than two in three American adults are considered to be overweight or obese. This is caused by many different factors, including lack of exercise.

Regular movement reduces blood pressure and strengthens the heart. By increasing bone density, it makes bones stronger and less likely to break. It improves blood cholesterol levels, which allows the cardiovascular system to work efficiently and reduces the risk of heart disease. Movement strengthens the body's immune system.

[
How do you feel after you
go for a walk or a run?
]

Movement is beneficial for a person's mental health—it reduces stress, anxiety, and depression. So get up and move!

To better understand how the body moves, you must first investigate how these different body systems work while the body is at rest. These basics, such as the body's structure, chemical reactions, energy generation, and the principles of matter in motion, form the necessary foundation for understanding human movement.

In this book, you will learn the basic anatomy of the human body and how bones, muscles, tendons, and nerves work together to make movement possible. We'll take a look at how our organs are involved in movement and what we can do to keep our bodies healthy and fit. Ready, set, let's move!

VOCAB LAB

Write down what you think each of the following words means. What root words can you find for help?

kinesiology, **cardiovascular**, **neuromuscular**, **mass**, **bone density**, **tendon**, **mechanical load**, **force**, **inertia**, **shear force**, **torsion**, and **tension**.

Compare your definitions with those of your friends or classmates. Did you all come up with the same meanings? Turn to the text and glossary if you need help.

KEY QUESTIONS

- Why is the study of human movement important?
- How has kinesiology affected your life?
- How do you use the different forces and mechanical loads to do the activities you love most?

Chapter One ▶
The Skeleton

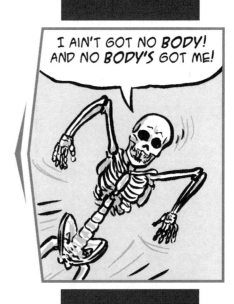

What functions does the skeletal system serve?

THE FIRST THING TO LEARN ABOUT MOVEMENT IS THE FRAMEWORK OF OUR BODIES.

LIKE THE FRAMES OF HOUSES, OUR SKELETONS GIVE SUPPORT AND STRUCTURE TO OUR BODIES. WE WOULDN'T BE ABLE TO MOVE AN INCH WITHOUT IT.

ARE YOU GOING TO DO THAT BONE THING AGAIN?

WHY DO YOU ASK?

Your skeletal system provides the scaffolding for your muscles, tendons, and ligaments, and even for your organs. Your skeleton is essential to your ability to move!

From the top of your head to the tips of your toes, your bones provide support for your body. Together, the bones of the skeletal system create the base framework of the body. Other tissues and organs attach to the skeleton, giving shape to the human body.

Bones do more than provide a frame—they enclose and protect the spinal cord, brain, heart, and many other organs. Bone marrow, found inside your bones, produces the red and white blood cells that your body needs to carry oxygen and fight infection.

BONE BASICS

With 206 bones, the human skeleton is the basic frame of the body. Bones begin to develop before birth and continue to grow through adulthood. When bones first form, they are made of cartilage, a firm tissue that is softer and more flexible than bone. Newborn infants are very flexible because many of their bones are still made of cartilage.

Within a few weeks of birth, the bones begin the process of ossification, or the formation of bone. During ossification, the cartilage is replaced by hard deposits of calcium phosphate and collagen, the two main components of bone. Ossification continues through childhood into early adulthood.

When you are a child, your bones are small, but they grow longer as you become an adult. The lengthening of bones is called longitudinal growth. Longitudinal growth occurs because the bones of children and teens have growth plates. Growth plates have columns of cartilage cells that grow in length before turning into hard, mineralized bone. When doctors X-ray a child's bones, they can easily find the growth plates and even use these to approximate a child's age. Longitudinal growth generally ends in the later teen years, when you reach your full adult height. Sometimes bones grow in diameter, called circumferential growth. This type of growth can occur throughout your lifetime.

Bone tissue constantly remodels throughout your lifetime. In this process, old bone is resorbed and new bone is formed. Resorption is the process of old bone tissue being broken down and digested by the body. This process is not the same in all bones and might occur more frequently in some bones than others. As long as a person is alive, their bones are constantly remodeling.

Bone growth and remodeling depend on specialized cells called osteocytes. There are two types of osteocytes—osteoblasts and osteoclasts. These cells are responsible for remodeling and forming new bone. Osteoblasts form new bone and are often found on the surface of new bone. Osteoclasts are large cells that dissolve and resorb old or damaged bone tissue.

MOTION NOTION

Osteoporosis is a disease that occurs when bones become weak because resorption happens more than new bone is made. The bones break easily because there is less bone tissue.

WHAT ARE BONES MADE OF?

Have you ever heard the saying that something is as strong as bone? Bones are some of the strongest, hardest structures in your body. Several minerals, including calcium, phosphorus, and sodium, make bones hard and strong. Calcium, in the form of the chemical compounds calcium carbonate and calcium phosphate, makes up about 60 to 70 percent of bone's weight. The amount of these calcium compounds in a bone determines the bone's stiffness and its compressive strength, which is its ability to resist being squeezed or shortened.

> Do your parents ever tell you to drink your milk? Milk contains calcium—your parents are helping you strengthen your bones!

Bones also contain a protein called collagen. Collagen gives bone its flexibility and ability to resist the pulling force of tension. Bones even contain water, which delivers nutrients and remove wastes from bone tissue. A healthy bone has about 25 to 30 percent of its weight in water. As a bone's water content decreases, it becomes more brittle and breaks more easily.

A bone is made of two types of tissue—cortical bone and cancellous bone. Cortical bone is very dense. It is found in the shafts of long bones and in the exterior of bones. Cortical bone can withstand heavy loads and muscle tension force before it fails and breaks.

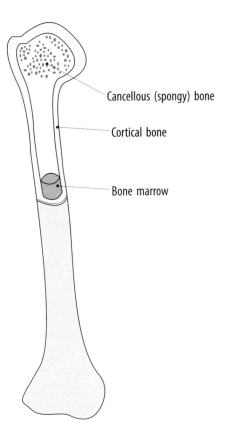

Cancellous (spongy) bone

Cortical bone

Bone marrow

MOTI N TION

Porosity is the number of cavities, or pores, in a bone. Porosity determines a bone's strength. A bone that is porous has less calcium carbonate and calcium phosphate. The more porous a bone is, the weaker it is.

About 80 percent of the human skeleton is cortical bone. Although it looks solid, cortical bone actually has many passageways for blood vessels and nerves.

Inside cortical bone, cancellous bone is a mesh-like network of tiny spaces and bone pieces called trabeculae. Cancellous bone is less dense than cortical bone, making it weaker and less stiff. This porous bone tissue can absorb energy and distribute loads that are applied to the skeleton. The bone marrow found within cancellous bone produces red and white blood cells.

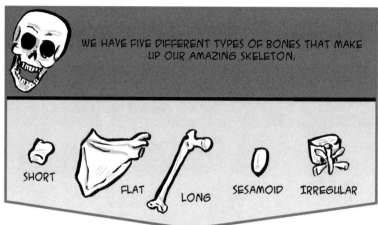

FIVE TYPES OF BONES

Not all bones look the same. Some are short, while others are flat or long. The bones in your body can be grouped into five categories by shape—short, flat, long, sesamoid, and irregular. Short bones are small, solid, and often shaped like a cube. The bones in the wrist, (carpals) and the ankle, (tarsals) are short bones. They provide stability and allow some movement.

Flat bones are generally flat or slightly curved. They might vary in thickness. Flat bones protect the body's organs like shields. The ribs and sternum in the chest are flat bones that protect the heart. The ilium bone, which forms the upper part of the pelvis, the clavicle (collar bone), and scapula (shoulder blade) are all flat bones. The skull, protecting the brain, is made up of flat bones. In addition to protecting organs, flat bones provide a large area for muscles to attach. Many of these bones form the axial skeleton, the central part of the skeleton.

Long bones provide the main support of the appendicular skeleton. These are the bones that attach to the axial skeleton.

BONE MARROW

Inside many bones, the blood cells needed throughout the body are made in the soft bone marrow. Stem cells there produce red blood cells that carry oxygen to the body's tissues. Bone marrow also produces platelets, which help with blood clotting when a person has a cut or wound. Some types of white blood cells, which help the body fight infection, are also produced in the bone marrow.

Long bones have a long shaft with two ends. The longest bone in the body, the femur in the leg, is a long bone. The small finger bones are also long bones. Many long bones support the body's weight and help it move. Other long bones include the rest of the leg bones (fibula and tibia) and arms (radius, ulna, humerus). While all bones contain bone marrow, the bone marrow in long bones can help the body survive extreme cases of hunger and blood loss.

Sesamoid bones are small, round bones embedded in tendons. They are often found in the tendons of the hands, feet, and knees. Sesamoid bones protect tendons from stress and wear. The kneecap (patella) is the largest and most well-known sesamoid bone.

Some bones don't fit into any category. These irregular bones vary in shape, size, and structure. Often, muscles and other soft tissues that attach to and apply force to a bone affect its shape. The vertebrae that protect the spinal cord are an example of irregular bones. They form a tunnel around the spinal cord. The vertebrae have several protrusions where muscles, tendons, and ligaments attach to them. Other irregular bones include the coccyx and sacrum in the tailbone and the ischium and pubis in the pelvis.

Bones increase in size from the top of the body to the bottom, depending on how much body weight they bear. Thus, the bones of the legs, pelvis, and lower back are larger than bones in the arms and upper chest.

JOINTS AND MOVEMENT

Bones are very strong. But if all of the skeleton's bones were fused together, it would be very difficult to move! To solve this problem, the skeleton has joints, the places where two bones meet.

Joints are where bones come together. They also allow the body to move in many ways. Without joints, you would not be able to bend your arm or type with your fingers. Joints allow you to curl your toes and lift your legs.

[Not all joints move the same way or have the same range of motion.]

Some joints move freely, while others move just a little bit and some do not move at all. Some joints open and close like a hinge while others allow more complex movement. Notice how your shoulder or hip joints allow movement backward, forward, and sideways. Joints can be classified according to how much movement they allow and in what direction.

Some joints are fixed and do not move. In adults, the joints between the skull bones are examples of immovable joints. The skull is made of bony plates that protect the brain. A thin layer of fibrous connective tissue called a suture joins these plates together very tightly so they do not move. Many joints in your face are also fixed.

Other joints move slightly. These joints are connected by cartilage or slightly flexible ligaments. The disks between the vertebrae are an example of this type of joint. They connect each vertebra in the spinal column and allow for slight movement. Each vertebra in the spine moves a little in relation to the bone above and below it.

ARE YOU DOUBLE JOINTED?

Have you ever heard someone claim that they are double jointed? Maybe they can bend their fingers or rotate their arms into positions that seem impossible. How can they do this? The answer generally involves flexibility. Flexibility is how much the body's soft tissue can be extended. The joints are held together by ligaments and other soft tissues. These tissues can vary from person to person in the amount of support they provide and how much they stretch. A person who says they are double jointed is probably just very flexible and has loose joints!

> Together, these small movements give the spine its flexibility.

Most joints in the body are freely moveable. Able to move in many directions, these joints, sometimes called synovial joints, form where two bones are joined together by ligaments. Cartilage cushions the end of each bone, and a membrane-lined cavity filled with synovial fluid lubricates and cushions the joint. Joints at your elbows, shoulders, and ankles are examples of moveable joints.

Three main types of moveable joints have big roles in voluntary movement. Hinge joints allow movement in one direction. Joints at the knees and elbows are examples of hinge joints. You can bend and straighten your knee, but you cannot move it sideways. Pivot joints perform a rotating or twisting motion. A pivot joint at the top of the vertebral column allows you to move your head from side to side. In a ball-and-socket joint, the round end of a long bone fits into a depression called a socket in another bone. This type of joint can move in all directions and can rotate. Joints at the hip and shoulder are ball-and-socket joints.

HOLDING IT ALL TOGETHER

Although many bones fit together well at a joint, this connection alone is not stable enough to allow you to walk, run, and move. Think about a small stack of blocks. Each piece fits well against the one above and below it. But if you try to move or bend the stack, the entire column falls apart. Now image if you put a large rubber band around the blocks. Could you more easily manipulate the blocks without them falling apart?

MOTION NOTION

A bursa is a synovial fluid-filled sac that helps to reduce the friction between a bone and a tendon or a bone and a muscle.

WHAT IS CARTILAGE?

Cartilage is a flexible, rubbery substance that is more flexible than bone, but firmer than muscle. Can you feel how the bridge of your nose is stiff and inflexible, while the end of your nose wiggles? Can you feel how you can bend your upper ears? Cartilage gives these body parts structure and flexibility. Cartilage is also found in between bones, where it supports the bones and protects them from rubbing against each other.

THE HEAD BONE'S CONNECTED TO THE . . .

An adult human has 206 bones in its skeletal system. The skeleton provides a scaffolding for the muscles and organs to remain secure and protected. You can learn more about the different bones in the body at this interactive website.

 inner body skeletal system

In a similar way, connective tissues, which include tendons, ligaments, and joint capsules, provide the extra support the skeleton needs for movement. A tendon is a soft tissue that connects a muscle to a bone. When the tendon of a muscle crosses a joint, there will be movement at that joint when the muscle contracts. The movement created when a muscle contracts depends on the size and length of the tendon, as well as the type of joint.

Ligaments are bands of dense, fibrous tissue that connect two bones and hold each bone in its place. Joint capsules surround a joint and enclose the joint cavity with a membrane, which holds protective synovial fluid. When the two bones that connect at a joint move, they can rub and cause friction. Too much friction will wear away the cushioning cartilage at the end of each bone, which causes a lot of pain. The synovial fluid in the joint capsule helps protect the joint and its cartilage from friction.

Along with providing support to the joints, tendons and ligaments help the body move. When a muscle contracts, it generates a force. The tendons and ligaments deliver this force to the bone, which makes it move. As the bone moves, tendons and ligaments stretch. Typically, after stretching, they return to their normal length. If they stretch too far or too often, tendons and ligaments can become loose, which affects their ability to protect and stabilize a joint. In some cases, the ligaments become unable to return to their normal length and require surgery.

JOINT STABILITY

Have you ever sprained your knee? This can happen if the joint is not stable. When joints are stable, bones move smoothly without popping out of place. Factors that affect a joint's stability include its shape and the soft tissue supporting it. The shape of the bone is a major factor in a joint's stability. Typically, bones that connect at a joint are shaped as opposites. When one bone ends in a socket, the connecting bone ends in a ball.

The more the bones are in contact, the more stable the joint will be. The amount of surface area contact between bones at a joint differs for each person. That is why some people are more likely to have joint problems than others. In addition, joints are generally more stable in certain positions where the most amount of each bone is in contact with the other.

[When bones are in positions with less contact, they are less stable and more susceptible to injury.]

MOTION NOTION

The range of motion (ROM) of a joint describes its flexibility and is a measure of how far the joint can stretch and reach. Joint ROM is measured in degrees.

Every bone has a modeling threshold. The modeling threshold determines how much force can be applied to the bone before the bone begins to change and adapt. When a bone experiences forces greater than its modeling threshold, it can stimulate new bone development. New bone formation can enhance mineralization, adding osteocyte bone cells. Bones that experience greater forces are often larger or denser than bones that do not experience the same forces. For example, runners often have higher bone density in their leg bones because these bones are subjected to increased force during running workouts. This is one way exercise is good for your bones!

The arrangement and strength of muscles, ligaments, and tendons also affect a joint's stability. When muscles have enough strength and length, the joint is more stable. However, if the muscles are imbalanced around a joint, one muscle may exert too much force on the joint. This can cause the joint to become less stable. For example, if the thigh's quadriceps muscles are stronger than its hamstring muscles, this imbalance might cause the knee joint to move beyond its normal range of motion.

In addition, the length of the muscle can impact a joint's stability. If a muscle has limited flexibility, it will not be able to put the joint in the appropriate position. This can affect the joint's stability.

During a person's lifetime, ligaments and tendons can shrink or get longer, depending on how they are used. When ligaments change, the joint can become less stable. For example, if a person sprains their wrist, the ligaments stretch and loosen. The loose ligaments make the wrist less stable and at higher risk of another injury.

For the body to move, the individual structures—bones, tendons, ligaments, and cartilage—must all function properly and work together.

KEY QUESTIONS

- **What are the different types of bones and their uses?**
- **What are the different types of joints? What kinds of motion does each type make possible?**
- **Why do we have different types of bones and joints? How would our bodies be different if all bones and joints were the same?**

BUILD A MODEL OF THE ARM

The arm is made of three main bones: the humerus, ulna, and radius. These bones support the arm and provide attachment points for the muscles that move the arm. Joints at the shoulder and elbow give the arm a wide range of motion and flexibility. In this project, you will build a model of an arm and recreate its movement.

- **Research the bones of the arm and how they are organized.** This website is a good place to start.

  🔍 Inner Body bones of arm hand

  - How is the arm made?

  - What is the function of each of its bones?

  - How does it move?

- **Create a model of the arm, including the shoulder and elbow joints.**

  - What types of materials can you use to create your model?

  - What type of joints are at the shoulder and elbow?

  - What type of motion does each joint allow?

To investigate more, consider that several types of injuries can affect the movement of the arm and its joints. How would a bone injury affect the arm? How would a joint injury inhibit movement of the arm? Create an injury to your arm model and demonstrate its effect on movement.

HA! FINALLY GOT IT TO WORK!

WHAT MAKES BONES STRONG?

Bones are both strong and flexible. The strength of a bone depends on the amount of the mineral calcium carbonate it contains. In this experiment, you will test how calcium carbonate affects bone strength. The next time you have a chicken for dinner, save the bones for your experiments.

- **Put a chicken bone in a glass filled with vinegar, covering it completely.** Cover the top of the glass with plastic wrap. Let the bone soak for three or four days.

- **Remove the bone from the vinegar and dry it.** Try to bend it. What happens? How does the bone feel? Does the bone bend easily?

- **Try bending a chicken bone of the same size and shape that hasn't been soaking in vinegar.** How are they the same? How are they different?

- **How do you explain the difference between the two bones?** Research what is happening to the bone. What is the effect of vinegar on calcium carbonate? What does this mean for bones?

> To investigate more, repeat the experiment while changing some of the variables, such as the time the bone soaks in vinegar, the type of bone used, and even the type of vinegar used. How do these changes affect your results? Create a chart or other visual way to present your results.

VOCAB LAB

Write down what you think each of the following words means. What root words can you find for help?

ossification, osteocytes, resorption, cortical bone, cancellous bone, flat bones, long bones, synovial joint, pivot joint, hinge joint, ball-and-socket joint, and **stability**.

Compare your definitions with those of your friends or classmates. Did you all come up with the same meanings? Turn to the text and glossary if you need help.

Chapter Two ▶

The Muscular System

What causes your muscles to contract and how do they move your body?

Muscles provide the power and force needed to move your skeleton. They control your body's movement!

While your bones support your body, your muscles control your movement. They provide the force and power needed to move your bones and body. When you sit in a chair, shoot a basketball, or turn your head, muscles make it happen. Even when you are perfectly still, muscles in your body are constantly moving.

Muscles help the body perform the necessary functions to live. Muscles enable the heart to beat, the blood vessels to regulate blood pressure and flow in the body, and the chest to rise and fall in breathing. Muscles even help you communicate, moving your mouth and tongue to talk or making expressions on your face.

There are more than 600 muscles in the human body. About half a person's body weight is muscle. Many muscles connect to bones with the tough, cord-like tissues called tendons. Not all muscles are the same, however.

TYPES OF MUSCLES

In the human body, there are three main types of muscles: skeletal muscle, smooth or involuntary muscle, and cardiac muscle. Each has its own function and unique structure.

Skeletal muscles attach to bones in the legs, arms, abdomen, chest, neck, and face. They hold the skeleton together, which gives the body its shape and moves all the different parts of the skeleton. Skeletal muscles move your legs when you walk, move your arms when you catch a ball, and move your fingers when you write. They are sometimes called voluntary muscles because a person can control when and how they move.

Skeletal muscles are made of long cells called muscle fibers that can contract quickly and powerfully. When looked at under a microscope, the fibers that make up skeletal muscles have horizontal stripes, giving the muscle a striated appearance.

Smooth muscles, also called involuntary muscles, are automatically controlled by the body's nervous system.

[
A person does not have to think about contracting these involuntary muscles because the nervous system does it for them.
]

For example, the smooth muscles of your stomach and intestines work all day to digest food without a thought from you. Smooth muscles are often found in the walls of hollow organs. They can be found in the digestive system, blood vessels, bladder, airways, and the uterus.

MOTION NOTION

The striated appearance of skeletal muscle is caused by bands of actin and myosin filaments. These are proteins that form the sarcomeres, or the basic units, of the muscle.

Fascicles are bundles of muscle fibers. A fascicle may hold as many as 200 muscle fibers. The fascicle is covered with a connective sheath called the perimysium. It protects the muscle fibers and provides a path for nerves and blood vessels. It also helps with force transmission.

Smooth muscles can stretch and maintain tension for long periods of time. The autonomic nervous system sends a message for the smooth muscle to contract, which allows the organs to expand and relax as needed. For example, the walls of the stomach and intestines are made of smooth muscles, which work to break up food and move it through the body's digestive system. Smooth muscles are also in the walls of blood vessels, where they expand and contract to move blood through the vessels and help maintain blood pressure. In the eye, smooth muscles change the shape of the lens to focus on objects.

Smooth muscles take longer to contract than skeletal muscles, but can stay contracted for long periods of time because they do not tire easily. Smooth muscles are also made of fibers, but they don't appear striated—they look smooth under a microscope.

Cardiac muscle is located in the heart. The walls of the heart's four chambers are almost entirely made up of cardiac muscle fibers. Like smooth muscle, cardiac muscle is involuntary. It contracts when it receives a signal to make a heartbeat. The heart's powerful contractions pump blood out of the heart.

THE MAKE-UP OF SKELETAL MUSCLE

Like every other tissue in your body, muscles are made of individual cells. Muscle cells are called fibers and are shaped like long, thin cylinders. Individual muscle fibers join together into bundles called a fascicle. Thousands of fascicles join together to form a muscle. All of a muscle's fascicles work together to contract at the same time and produce movement.

When stimulated, a muscle contracts to produce motion. Contraction occurs when a nerve impulse triggers the muscle to move. The muscle relaxes when the impulse is removed. This cycle of contraction and relaxation creates all of the movement in your body. The part of your body that moves depends on where the muscle is attached. A muscle attached to the leg bone will move the leg when stimulated. It cannot move the finger bones because it is not attached to them.

Most skeletal muscles are attached to a bone at two or more places. The origin of a muscle is a fixed attachment that does not move. At the opposite end of the muscle is what's called an insertion point. The insertion point is an attachment on a bone that usually moves during an action. For example, the upper arm bone, or the humerus, has a large muscle called the biceps brachii on it. The biceps muscle's origin point is at the scapula, while its insertion point is on the radius bone of the forearm. When the biceps muscle contracts, it moves the radius bone. The scapula and upper arm, or the origin, do not move.

WORKING IN PAIRS

Just as the individual fibers and fascicles in a muscle work together, individual muscles also have to work together. When a muscle moves, it contracts in one direction. Your biceps muscle contracts and pulls your forearm toward it. But how does your forearm return to its original position? The biceps muscle cannot move it in the opposite direction. Instead, a partner muscle located in the back of the upper arm, called the triceps, contracts and pulls it back.

MOTION IN MOTION

While some muscles attach directly to a bone, many muscles are attached to a bone with a tendon. The tendon transfers the force generated by the muscle's contraction to the bone.

Like the biceps and triceps of the upper arm, many muscles work together in pairs. When one muscle in a pair contracts, the other muscle stretches or relaxes.

A contraction that shortens a muscle is called concentric, while a contraction that lengthens a muscle is eccentric.

[This working relationship is like two people sawing down a tree with a long, flat saw.]

The first side pulls the saw while the second side stretches. Then it reverses, with the second side pulling hard on the saw while the first side stretches.

One muscle in the pair is the agonist, while the other muscle is the antagonist. The agonist is the primary mover. When the agonist contracts, it causes a particular movement. At the same time, the antagonist performs the opposite action of the agonist. If the agonist contracts, the antagonist relaxes. In the upper arm, the biceps contracts to move the forearm. Because the biceps produces the movement of the arm, it is the agonist. When it contracts, the triceps muscle relaxes. When the triceps contracts, it pulls the forearm back to its original position. The biceps relaxes.

A MUSCLE CONTRACTS AND MOVES IN ONE DIRECTION, BUT A DIFFERENT ONE NEEDS TO ACT AGAINST IT.

THIS IS CALLED *AGONIST MOVEMENT*. YOUR ARM IS A GREAT EXAMPLE! WHEN THE BICEPS CONTRACTS, YOUR ARM MOVES UP. WHEN YOUR TRICEPS CONTRACTS, IT MOVES BACK DOWN AND RELAXES YOUR BICEPS.

BICEPS

TRICEPS

Muscles working in pairs create paired movements. An example of paired movements is flexion and extension. Flexion is a decrease in the angle between two bones, such as when the elbow bends and the angle between the humerus (upper arm) and the radius (forearm) gets smaller. The opposite of flexion is extension, the increase in an angle between two bones. Straightening a bent elbow is an example of extension, increasing the angle between the two arm bones. The muscles in the arm, the triceps and biceps, work together to bend and unbend the arm at the elbow. The triceps extends the elbow, while the biceps flexes it.

Abduction and adduction are another type of paired movement. These movements are typically side-to-side, like moving the arm away from and toward the body during a jumping jack. Abduction movement occurs when the arm moves away from the body. Its opposite is adduction, the moving toward the body.

WORKING ALONE

Not all skeletal muscles work in pairs. Muscles called synergists work with agonists to help them contract efficiently. Synergists provide additional pulling force at a muscle's insertion site to start a muscle movement. Synergists also provide stability at a muscle's point of origin to control movement. Like a supporting actor in a play or movie, the synergist has a smaller, but important, part in muscle movement.

One example of a synergist muscle is the brachialis. The brachialis is a smaller muscle located underneath the biceps on the upper arm. The biceps attaches to the radius in the lower arm, while the brachialis attaches to another bone of the lower arm, the ulna. When it contracts, the brachialis helps the biceps move the lower arm.

MOTION NOTION

Most of the skeletal bones in the body move using muscle pairs. When the agonist flexes, the antagonist stretches. The agonist moves a bone in one direction, the antagonist moves it in the opposite direction.

HOW MUSCLES CONTRACT

Contraction is the basic action of any muscle. When you think about moving your leg, your brain sends a message through the nervous system to tell your leg muscles to contract. The muscles can contract with different amounts of force, depending on the message that the nervous system sends. The muscle's structure is a key piece to how contraction takes place.

Each muscle fiber is made of many long myofibrils, which are cylinders of muscle proteins. These delicate, rod-like strands run the total length of the muscle. Hundreds or thousands of myofibrils exist in each muscle fiber. Each myofibril is made up of smaller, individuals units of contracting tissue called sarcomeres, which are stacked end to end.

Each sarcomere connects to another sarcomere by a connective tissue called the Z line, which helps to give the sarcomeres stability. A sarcomere begins at one Z line and ends at the next Z line. The sarcomere is where the muscle's contraction occurs.

The sarcomere contains thread-like proteins called myofilaments. There are two major types of myofilaments: thick (myosin) and thin (actin). Muscle contraction occurs when these protein filaments slide over one another.

Myosin is a protein that generates force in a muscle contraction. A myosin filament has a head and a tail. The tails of about 300 myosin molecules form the shaft of a thick myosin filament. The heads of these myosin molecules project out toward the thin actin filaments.

A thin actin filament is made from two long chains of actin molecules twisted around each other. Each actin molecule has a binding site where a myosin head can attach.

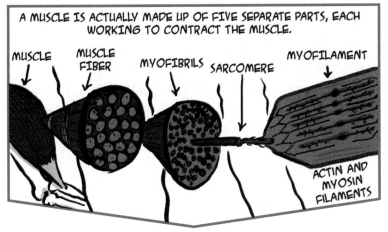

A MUSCLE IS ACTUALLY MADE UP OF FIVE SEPARATE PARTS, EACH WORKING TO CONTRACT THE MUSCLE.

MUSCLE

MUSCLE FIBER

MYOFIBRILS SARCOMERE

MYOFILAMENT

ACTIN AND MYOSIN FILAMENTS

WHEN YOU THINK ABOUT IT, OUR MUSCLES ARE REALLY COMPLEX ORGANS WITH A LOT GOING ON.

Because the attraction between myosin heads and the actin binding sites is so strong, long filaments called tropomyosin loop around the actin to cover the binding sites and prevent unwanted muscle contraction. In a skeletal muscle, myosin and actin fibers are organized in a repeating structure. Each thick filament is surrounded by several thin filaments.

Voluntary muscle contraction begins when the brain sends an electrical signal through the nervous system to the motor unit in the muscle.

The motor units relay the signal to the muscle fibers that they are connected to, which triggers the release of calcium from the sarcoplasmic reticulum. The calcium binds to troponin, a protein in the muscle that helps to hold tropomyosin in place over the actin binding sites. The calcium causes the troponin to change its shape. As it changes shape, the troponin pulls tropomyosin away from the binding sites. Now the myosin heads can attach to the actin filaments.

A smile uses 17 different muscles in the face, while a frown requires even more—43 muscles.

MOTION NOTION

The bond between actin
and myosin is so strong that
the muscle needs energy to
break the bond and repeat
the contraction sequence.

A muscle contracts when all of the sarcomeres in its myofibrils contract and shorten at the same time. To do this, the thick myosin filaments grab onto the thin actin filaments. The thick filaments pull the thin filaments past them, which shortens the sarcomere. The pulling action is like a rower moving an oar through the water to push the boat forward. As long as there is energy to power this process, the thick myosin filaments will repeatedly pull the thin filaments, causing the muscle contraction.

To avoid fatigue, not all muscle fibers contract at the same time. Some contract, while others relax. As the contracting fibers become fatigued, the resting fibers take over the work. The muscle's fibers switch back and forth, constantly sharing the workload.

FAST, SLOW, OR IN-BETWEEN

Sometimes you need to sprint down the street. You need an intense burst of force for a short period of time. Another day, you might want to take a long walk, needing your muscles to move for a longer period of time. A muscle's performance can be described by force and endurance. Force is the maximum contraction strength of the muscle. Endurance is the amount of time the muscle can maintain a contraction. Some activities, such as lifting a heavy weight or running a short sprint, require an intense burst of force. Other activities, such as biking a long distance or running a marathon, require muscles to contract with lesser force for a longer time. Differences in muscle fibers allow your body to move both ways.

Muscle fibers can be slow, fast, or intermediate. A fiber's twitch is a description of the speed and frequency of the neural signal passing through its motor unit. Each person is born with a varying amount of slow- and fast-twitch muscle fibers.

Have you noticed your friend might be really fast at sprinting, but you are faster at running a 5K, which requires more endurance? Most people have a combination of slow- and fast-twitch muscle fibers, which allows them to perform different sporting activities.

Fast fibers generate a lot of force, but also tire easily. They are meant to produce quick, strong contractions that do not last very long. Fast fibers are good for anaerobic exercise, such as sprinting or weightlifting. The nerve connecting to these fibers is large and needs a large stimulus from the brain before it fires. This large nerve connects to thousands of fibers. When it does fire, many fibers activate at the same time and generate a lot of force. Fast fibers contract rapidly and use up a lot of energy in a short time.

Slow fibers are not particularly fast, but can keep going for longer periods. Slow-twitch muscles are useful for aerobic activities that require endurance, including long-distance running and biking.

Some muscles have a higher percentage of slow-twitch fibers. For example, the soleus muscle in the lower leg helps a person stand. It has a higher proportion of slow fibers. This allows you to stand for hours. The nerves that connect to slow-twitch muscle fibers are small and fire with only a small stimulus from the brain. They connect to only a few fibers, which makes slow-twitch motor units good for fine motor skills, such as writing or blinking. Slow-twitch muscle fibers are generally smaller and weaker than fast-twitch fibers.

Intermediate fibers are a combination of fast and slow fibers. They contract quickly, but not quite as fast as fast fibers. They can sustain activity for longer than fast fibers, but not as long as slow fibers.

THE ROLE OF CALCIUM

Calcium is critical for making a muscle contract. Within the muscles, there is a system of storage units called the sarcoplasmic reticulum that store calcium. When they receive a signal, the sarcoplasmic reticulum release calcium, which spreads through the muscle and triggers a contraction.

MOTION NOTION

Endurance training can change fast fibers to be more like intermediate fibers, making them less easily tired.

MUSCLE PROPERTIES

Muscles produce the force needed for movement. But the type of force a muscle can produce depends on four properties: irritability, contractility, extensibility, and elasticity.

Irritability is a muscle's ability to respond to stimulation. This property determines how fast a muscle reacts and how strong a stimulus it needs to contract. To move, muscles must create tension. The ability to generate tension is a muscle's contractility. How hard a muscle contracts depends on the muscle's length, its timing, its motor units, and what joint it moves.

A muscle's extensibility is its ability to stretch beyond its normal length. For example, when a person bends a knee, the hamstring muscle in the back of the upper leg contracts and pulls the leg backward. At the same time, the quadriceps muscle on the front of the thigh stretches beyond its resting length.

After being stretched, a muscle's ability to return to its normal resting length is called its elasticity. Typically, muscles return to their normal length after being stretched. If they are stretched too far, the muscle fibers can tear, causing an injury called a muscle strain.

MOTION NOTION

Muscular dystrophy is an inherited group of diseases that affect the muscles, causing them to weaken and break down over time.

LEVERS FOR MOVEMENT

When muscles contract, they create force to move the weight of the body and its parts. On each end, skeletal muscles are attached to bone. When the muscles contract, the attachment causes the bones to move.

Muscles move bones using three different lever systems. A lever is a simple machine made with a rod that rotates around an axis, called a fulcrum. A lever system includes a force being applied, called effort, and an opposing force, called load, that you intend to move.

A teeter-totter is a simple example of a first-class lever. You sit on one end and push down, which is the effort, in order to move your friend sitting at the other end, which is acting as the load. The point where the teeter-totter rotates around is its fulcrum.

FIRST-CLASS LEVER

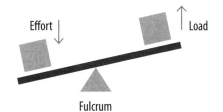

Effort

Load

Fulcrum

[The human body consists of many lever systems that are critical for movement.]

In your body, the bones act as levers, while the joints serve as the axis of rotation, or fulcrums. Your body itself or an object that you want to hold or lift acts as the load. Your head on the top of your body is an example of a first-class lever. The spine is the fulcrum, while the posterior neck muscles are the force, or effort. These muscles in the back of your neck move the front of your head, the load.

MUSCLES CREATE STABILITY

In addition to helping you move, muscles provide stability. Sometimes, when a muscle contracts, the attached joint does not move or moves only a tiny amount. This is called static muscle activity. It provides support for the joint or minimizes movement caused by an external force.

MOTION NOTION

The largest and strongest muscle in your body is the gluteus maximus, while the smallest skeletal muscle is the stapedius, which is located in your middle ear. Where do you think the gluteus maximus is located?

VOCAB LAB

Write down what you think each of the following words means. What root words can you find for help?

skeletal muscle, **smooth muscle**, **cardiac muscle**, **voluntary muscle**, **involuntary muscle**, **fibers**, **fascicle**, **contraction**, **insertion**, **origin**, **antagonist**, **agonist**, **synergist**, **myofibrils**, **sarcomere**, **actin**, **myosin**, **tropomyosin**, **Z line**, and **troponin**.

Compare your definitions with those of your friends or classmates. Did you all come up with the same meanings? Turn to the text and glossary if you need help.

In a second-class lever, the load sits between the effort and the fulcrum. A second-class lever allows you to move a relatively large load with a small amount of force. A wheelbarrow is an example of a second-class lever system. The wheel is the fulcrum, while the weight being lifted is the load and you apply the effort to move the load.

In the body, standing on the ball of your foot is an example of a second-class lever. The ball of your foot serves as the fulcrum and the weight of your body is the load. When your calf muscles contract, they create a lifting force that allows you to lift your body.

SECOND-CLASS LEVER

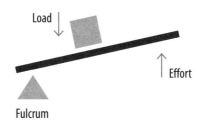

[
In your body, third-class levers are the most common.
]

In a third-class lever, the force is applied between the load and the fulcrum. A broom is an example of a third-class lever. Your hand at the top of the broom is the fulcrum. Your other hand placed in the middle of the broom applies the force, which moves the load— the broom itself.

THIRD-CLASS LEVER

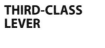

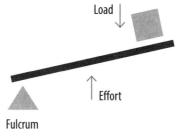

Your arm is an example of a third-class lever system. When you want to lift a heavy object or load, your elbow serves as a fulcrum. Your biceps muscles exert force onto the lower arm, which causes rotation around the elbow joint and allows you to lift the object.

HOW MUCH FORCE?

The amount of force needed to move a load depends on the distances between the effort, the fulcrum, and the load. The distance between the effort and the fulcrum is known as the force arm, or FA. The longer the FA, the less force is needed to move the object. In addition, the distance between the load and the fulcrum, called the resistance arm, or RA, also affects the force needed. The longer the RA, the more force needed to move the object.

In your arm, the biceps muscle is attached to the radius bone only a few inches away from the elbow joint. Because this distance is so small, moving the elbow requires a great deal of force. That is why the human body must be strong to carry out daily tasks.

In human movement, many activities involve several different levers acting at the same time. For example, when you walk, levers in your toes, ankles, knees, and hips work together to perform the movement smoothly. Each lever must perform its own function while allowing the others to perform their functions.

ACTION POTENTIAL

The signal to contract that moves from a motor neuron to the muscle is called an action potential. The size of the action potential and resulting muscle contraction depend on the number of fibers in the motor unit. A stronger, more forceful movement requires a larger number of motor units to be activated.

KEY QUESTIONS

- Why do most muscles work in pairs?
- What are the three main types of muscles? How do they work?
- How do muscles work on bones to create movement?

BUILD A WORKING HAND MODEL

There are more than 30 muscles in your hand and forearm that work together to move your fingers, hand, and wrist. These muscles give your hand its flexibility and control for fine motor activities, such as drawing or writing. Your hand muscles also give you the grip strength that is needed for activities such as typing, picking up a glass of water, and gripping a baseball. In this activity, you'll create a working model of the hand and see how the muscles in your hands work together to help you move your fingers.

- **Research the bones and muscles of the hand and wrist.**

 anatomy explorer hand and wrist

  - How are the hand and fingers constructed?

  - What is the function of each of its bones?

  - What muscles are in the hand?

  - How are the hand's muscles attached to the bones?

  - How does it move?

- **Create a model of the hand, including the thumb and each finger.**

  - What type of joints and how many are in each finger?

  - What type of motion does each joint allow?

  - How do the hand's muscles create movement?

  - Where do the tendons attach the muscles to bone?

  - What materials are best for creating replicas of these muscles, bones, and tendons?

To investigate more, consider that injury to the muscles can affect movement in the wrist and hand. How would a muscle or tendon injury affect the hand and movement? Create an injury to your hand model and demonstrate its effect on movement.

WORKING IN PAIRS

Many of the muscles in your body work in pairs. A muscle only contracts and pulls, it cannot expand and push. Therefore, a muscle that pulls a joint cannot push it back in the opposite direction. It needs a partner, another muscle or muscle group that pulls the joint the other way to straighten the joint. In many muscle pairs, one muscle is stronger than the other muscle. In this activity, you will test the strength of several muscle pairs in your body.

- **Research different muscle pairs in your body.**

  - What muscle pairs did you find?

     anatomy explorer muscular system

  - Where are they located in the body?

  - What joints do they move?

  - In each pair, which muscle or muscle group do you predict will be stronger?

- **Using a spring scale, develop a way to test the strength of each pair of muscles.**

  - What did you discover?

  - If there is any difference in the muscle strength, how does this difference affect the movement of the joint?

  - Why do you think one muscle in a pair is stronger than the other? What purpose does it serve?

- **Create a chart, graph, or other visual presentation for your results.**

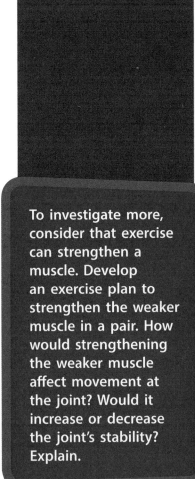

To investigate more, consider that exercise can strengthen a muscle. Develop an exercise plan to strengthen the weaker muscle in a pair. How would strengthening the weaker muscle affect movement at the joint? Would it increase or decrease the joint's stability? Explain.

FINDING LEVERS IN THE BODY

Muscles and bones act together as levers in your body. A lever is a simple machine that helps lift heavy objects with less effort. The object you lift might be your body itself or an item that you carry. A lever consists of a load (the object being lifted), a fulcrum (the point at which the lever rotates), and effort (the force applied to make the object move).

- **Levers are classified into three categories, depending on the position of the load, fulcrum, and effort.**

  - First-class lever: the fulcrum is between the force and the load.

  - Second-class lever: the load is between the fulcrum and the force.

  - Third-class lever: the force is between the fulcrum and the load.

- **Using your knowledge of levers, identify several muscle and bone levers in your body.**

  - What type of lever is it?

  - What is the fulcrum for this type of lever?

  - Where does the force in the lever come from?

- **Design a model of a lever system in your body to show how the bones and muscles work together to lift a heavy object.** Build a model of your lever system and test it. How heavy an object can you lift with your lever system?

WHAT LEVER CLASS IS MY SHOULDER?

To investigate more, create another model of a different lever system in your body. Compare the two systems. Can they both lift a heavy object? Or is one system better able to handle a heavy object? Why?

Chapter Three

The Brain-Body Connection

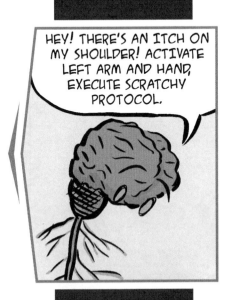

HEY! THERE'S AN ITCH ON MY SHOULDER! ACTIVATE LEFT ARM AND HAND, EXECUTE SCRATCHY PROTOCOL.

How does your brain control your body's movement?

The brain is a complex, powerful organ that constantly receives and sends signals to control the rest of the body.

Muscles work together to move the body. Simply walking down the street requires the coordination of muscles in the legs, arms, and torso, plus those that balance the body. As you walk up a hill, step over a rock, or climb stairs, your muscles adapt to the change in the environment and keep you moving.

How do all of your muscles know what to do? A master controller calls the shots behind every movement—the brain!

The brain is like the computer that controls all of the body's functions. It tells every part of the body what to do and when to do it. Most of the time, you are not even aware that the brain is sending out its commands, but it controls how you move every part of your body, from your head to your feet. The brain even controls movement that you aren't conscious of, such as your heart beating, eyelids blinking, and lungs breathing.

The body constantly sends signals to the brain about its environment. If you get near a hot fire, sensors in your skin send heat messages to your brain, which directs you to move your body away from the fire. Different sensors send information about pain, pressure, temperature, body position, and balance. These feedback systems are always supplying information to the brain.

> With the information from its feedback systems, the brain can direct the body to move appropriately.

THE NERVOUS SYSTEM

While the brain is like a computer controlling every part of the body, the nervous system is the body's communication network. When the brain's neurons send signals, they travel through the nervous system to other parts of the brain and the body. Electrical signals travel from the sense organs—the eyes, ears, and skin, for example—to the brain and back again through its network of neurons.

The nervous system has two main networks. The central nervous system (CNS) includes the brain and the spinal cord. The peripheral nervous system (PNS) is a complex network of nerves that spreads through the body. The CNS and PNS work together to send information throughout the body. If you want to move your arm, your brain sends a message down the spinal cord of the CNS to the PNS, which tells your arm to move.

MOTION

There are approximately 100 billion neurons in the human brain and an additional 13.5 million neurons in the spinal cord.

Messages are sent back to your brain the same way. Sensory input travels from receptor points throughout the body through the PNS to the brain. The brain processes and interprets the information in a fraction of a second, then makes a decision that is sent though the PNS to the muscles, which take the needed action.

SENDING SIGNALS

The primary cell involved in sending signals throughout the brain and nervous system is the neuron. Everything that happens in the brain is caused by neurons. Although neurons come in many shapes and sizes, most have the same basic structure. The neuron's cell body, or soma, contains its nucleus, which holds and makes the molecules that the neuron needs to live and function. Several dendrites stretch out from the cell like the branches of a tree.

Neurons don't touch each other. They are separated by spaces called synapses. To communicate, neurons send signals across the synapses by firing a chemical explosion from one neuron to the next.

Dendrites receive these chemical messages from other neurons. When a signal comes into a neuron from one of its dendrites, a chemical reaction begins in its nucleus, which causes electrical activity. If enough signals are received, a tiny blast called an action potential, or nerve impulse, travels into the neuron's axon and enters the axon terminal.

The axon terminal then releases a chemical called a neurotransmitter into the synapse. The neurotransmitter moves across the space and attaches to receptors on the dendrites of a nearby neuron. The next neuron sends the message from its dendrites down its cell body and the process continues again.

[
The human body holds billions of neurons. Neurons form connections with each other to allow messages to pass all around the body.
]

A neuron receives inputs from the neurons near it. If a neuron receives enough inputs, the stimulus will cause the neuron to fire a signal. If the inputs are not enough, the neuron will not fire and nothing will happen.

Not all neurons are the same. Some have specific functions. For example, sensory neurons pick up sensory information such as temperature or pain and pass it to the brain. Motor neurons send messages from the brain and nervous system to all of the body's muscles. Signals from motor neurons cause a person to throw a ball, hit a jump shot, or sit down.

Interneurons form bridges between sensory and motor neurons. They send messages between different parts of the nervous system. Quick movement, such as those controlled by reflexes, use interneurons. This would include pulling a hand away from something hot.

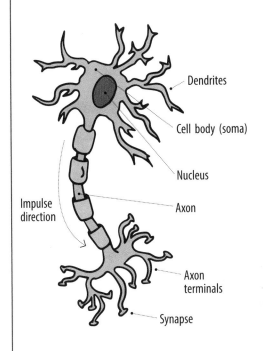

Dendrites

Cell body (soma)

Nucleus

Impulse direction

Axon

Axon terminals

Synapse

MOTION NOTION

There are lots of chemical neurotransmitters in the brain. Different neurotransmitters are used for different purposes. Some cause muscles to contract, while others cause nerves to excite or inhibit. Having different neurotransmitters allows the brain to send a variety of signals rather than using one type of signal to control everything.

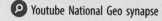
THE BRAIN: A CENTRAL HUB

For the body to move, the brain needs to send coordinated instructions to the body. The brain and the nervous system send a message to the muscles, causing them to contract and move. To do this, the brain needs to process all of the sensory information it receives from the body. Several areas of the brain are involved in processing this information.

The brain's outer layer is called the cerebral cortex. The cerebral cortex is the outer layer of the cerebrum, the major part of the brain where most of the brain's higher mental processing takes place. The cerebrum and cortex are divided into four parts, called lobes. Different brain functions happen in each lobe.

Most of the brain's information processing occurs in the cerebral cortex, which has a wrinkled surface. These folds expand its surface area, which increases the amount of information it can process.

The cerebral cortex has different sections involved with movement. The cerebral cortex perceives, analyzes, and responds to information from the outside world. It deals with sensory perception and processing, along with functions such as memory and decision-making. Within the cerebral cortex, the sensory cortex is located nearer the back of the brain and processes sensory information such as vision, taste, pain, temperature, and pressure. Near the middle of the brain, the motor cortex helps to coordinate and initiate movement.

At the base of the brain, the brain stem attaches the rest of the brain to the spinal cord. Without the brain stem, you wouldn't be alive—it is responsible for many of the body's most basic functions, such as breathing and swallowing. The brain stem controls your involuntary muscles, which move without you even thinking about it.

The brain stem tells the heart to beat fast or the stomach to digest food. It also acts as a relay station for the millions of messages that are sent between the brain and the body. A lot of control over motor movement occurs in the brain stem.

The cerebellum is attached to the brain stem at the back of the brain. It coordinates body movement, balance, and posture. When you hit a baseball or play the piano, the cerebellum activates. Without the cerebellum, you would not be able to stand upright, balance, and move around.

[Have you ever stood on one leg? Thank your cerebellum!]

The basal ganglia are three clusters of neurons at the base of the brain that work to initiate and integrate movement. The basal ganglia are important when learning motor tasks, such as throwing a ball or riding a bike. This area can smooth and adjust movements. For example, the basal ganglia can help you adjust your basketball jump shot when someone reaches in to try to block it.

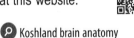

The brain is a very complex organ with lots of jobs! You can learn more about the anatomy and function of the brain at this website.

🔍 Koshland brain anatomy

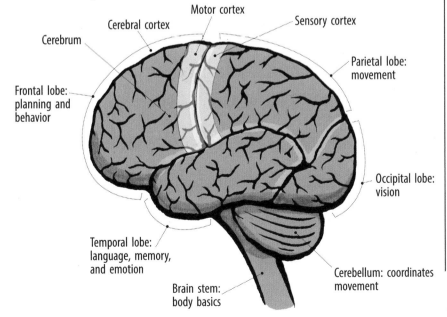

Motor cortex
Cerebral cortex
Sensory cortex
Cerebrum
Parietal lobe: movement
Frontal lobe: planning and behavior
Occipital lobe: vision
Temporal lobe: language, memory, and emotion
Cerebellum: coordinates movement
Brain stem: body basics

MOTOR NEURON DISEASE

Motor neuron diseases are a group of disorders that destroy motor neurons. When the signals between motor neurons are disrupted, the muscles do not work properly. They might develop uncontrollable twitching or stiffness. In some cases, movements become slow and require more effort. Gradually, the muscles can weaken and begin to waste away. Over time, the ability to control voluntary movement might also be lost. Amyotrophic lateral sclerosis (ALS), or Lou Gehrig's disease, is one type of motor neuron disease. ALS disrupts motor signals to all voluntary muscles, causing muscle weakness, which gradually affects how the body functions. In its later stages, ALS affects the motor neurons that control breathing and other important body functions, which leads to death.

The spinal cord is a group of neurons that run down the spine. The spinal cord's neurons carry messages from the brain to the muscles, and also carry signals from the body to the brain. When you want to move your arm, what happens? It's a complicated process that happens in an instant. The cerebral cortex sends messages to motor neurons in the spinal cord. The message to move your arm travels from the brain through the brain stem to the spinal cord. They tell the muscles to contract and move the arm.

The brain is divided into two hemispheres, right and left. The motor cortex on the left side of the brain controls the right side of the body, while the motor cortex on the brain's right side controls the left side of the body. For example, a message sent from the left motor cortex causes you to move your right arm.

The two hemispheres of the brain communicate by sending messages through the nerves of the corpus callosum, a highway of more than 200 nerve fibers that links the two hemispheres. Messages coming from the right side of the body cross to the left side of the brain and vice versa.

[
The brain and body are in constant communication.
]

As you walk, climb, jump, or perform any type of movement, your body's senses are continually sending messages to the brain about what they sense, both externally and internally. The brain processes and interprets these sensations and sends messages back that control movement. This constant communication is called a feedback loop.

YOUR NEURONS SEND THE MESSAGE TO THE RIGHT MUSCLES, BUT THEY ALSO TALK BACK!

YOUR SENSES AND BODY SYSTEMS ARE TALKING TO YOUR BRAIN AND SENDING INFORMATION— PAIN, HEAT, AND HOW FAR YOU SHOULD RUN!

KEEP IT UP!

THE BRAIN IS THE MASTER MIND, BUT WITHOUT THE FEEDBACK LOOP FROM THE SENSES, IT WOULD HAVE NO INFORMATION TO GET YOU HOME!

For example, when you go to walk up a set of stairs, your eyes send a message to the brain about the size of the step. The brain estimates the height of the step and sends a message to the muscles of the leg, which then lift the leg the appropriate amount.

If you misjudge the size of the step and move awkwardly, your senses send a message to the brain about your body position and the brain adjusts the leg movement needed for the next step so it goes more smoothly. Because your environment constantly changes as you move, this feedback loop is constantly sending signals, keeping you in the right place and position.

YOUR SENSES AND MOVEMENT

For the brain to send the right motor signals to the muscles, it must have information about the outside world. It gets that information from your senses. Through sight, hearing, touch, smell, and taste, your senses collect information about the world around you. The eyes, ears, skin, nose, and tongue receive stimuli, such as light and sound waves, pressure, or the touch of certain molecules.

MOTION NOTION

You can think of a feedback loop like a phone line, connecting multiple people so that they can send messages back and forth to each other.

Muscle spindles are sensory fibers in muscle that are key proprioceptors. They sense changes in the length and velocity of the muscle fibers. A tendon called the Golgi tendon organ is also an important proprioceptor, sensing the tension in a muscle.

Your brain engages with the outside world through these senses. Sensory neurons are special neurons in the sense organs that transform environmental stimuli into electrical signals. The sensory receptors send the electrical signals through the spinal cord to specialized areas of the cerebral cortex. There, they are processed into different sensations.

Our senses constantly gather information and send it to the brain. Most sensory signals remain unnoticed or unconscious. Unconscious sensations can still affect our actions and reactions, such as keeping our bodies balanced and upright.

KEEPING YOUR BALANCE

Have you ever closed your eyes and tried to touch your nose? How did you know where your nose was? How did you know where your arms and fingers were? Internal sensors called proprioceptors helped you figure it out! They give your brain a sense of position about your arms, legs, head, and trunk.

[Proprioception, or the sense of the body's position and movement in space, is sometimes called the sixth sense.]

Your muscles, tendons, joints, and ligaments hold your skeleton together. Proprioceptors in the muscles, tendons, joints, and ligaments monitor the changes in length, tension, and pressure that are linked to changes in position. Proprioceptors send electrical impulses via the sensory system to the brain for processing.

All of these sensors work together to create an unconscious image of the body's position in space. When the brain processes the signals, it can make a decision to change position or hold still, and then send a signal back to the muscles.

REFLEXES: AUTOMATIC MOVEMENT

When a thief breaks into a jewelry case that holds valuable diamonds, the store owner is relieved to know that the store's alarm system will automatically trigger, sounding the alarm and alerting the police. No decision needs to be made—it happens automatically. In the same way, your body has certain automatic movements that happen without thinking about them. These reflexes are designed to protect the body.

One such reflex, the stretch reflex, causes muscle contraction to prevent damage. In your muscles, sensory fibers called muscle spindles are mixed in with muscle fibers. The spindles sense the change in length and speed of muscle fibers. Stretching a muscle too rapidly can cause damage to the muscle and its tendons. When the spindles sense the muscle is stretching too quickly, the sensory nerves send a signal to the spinal cord and trigger a stretch reflex. A signal is sent right back to stimulate the muscle, causing the muscle to contract. At the same time, another signal goes to the opposite muscle to relax. This quick stretch reflex protects the muscle and tendon.

Has your doctor ever tapped your knee at the tendon? The tapping can trigger a small rapid stretch of your quadriceps muscle. What happens next? The rapid stretch of the quadriceps muscle triggers a reflex contraction, which causes your leg to kick out.

WARMING UP

When you warm up before an activity, you want to activate the muscles that you will be using. When getting ready to jump, doing mini jumps can activate the muscle spindles, which cause the muscles to contract. This gives you more activated muscle to use in your jumps, generating more force to help you jump high. On the other hand, stretching to warm up may have the opposite effect. Stretching before an activity can trigger the Golgi tendon reflex, which inhibits muscle firing and relaxes the muscles. Not having as many muscle fibers activated and firing results in less force in your muscle contractions. Not the best way to jump high!

Which is the best way to stretch your muscles? Should you hold a stretch or should you bounce it? Thinking about your reflexes might give you the answer. Both types of stretches activate a different reflex. During a hold stretch, the Golgi tendon reflex activates. Your muscle relaxes into a good stretch. In a bouncing stretch, the muscle spindles activate. What happens? The muscle contracts. Trying to stretch a contracting muscle can damage the muscle. So maybe a hold stretch is a better idea after all!

Another reflex is triggered by the Golgi tendon organs. The Golgi tendon organs carefully measure the amount of tension in a tendon that attaches a muscle to a bone. The Golgi tendon organs connect to sensory neurons that are connected to the central nervous system.

When you lift a heavy weight or stretch a muscle, the force pulls on the tendon, creating tension. If the weight is too heavy, the Golgi tendon reflex jumps into action to protect the muscle. It sends a signal to the central nervous system, which initiates several motor neurons to relax and lengthen the muscle. This action prevents further contraction, stops the risky movement, and protects the muscle from future damage. All of this takes place in a fraction of a second.

Try this to test your Golgi tendon reflex—stretch your hamstring and hold the stretch so that the muscle is in constant tension. Within about 20 seconds, do you feel your muscle start to relax? It's your Golgi tendon reflex at work!

The brain is a critical part of the body's ability to move. Without a brain, bodies wouldn't be able to function! In the next chapter, we'll take a look at another important component of human movement—the internal organs!

KEY QUESTIONS

- **What are the parts of the brain and what function does each part serve?**
- **How do neurons within the brain communicate? How does the brain communicate with the rest of the body?**

TEST YOUR REACTION SPEED

Quick! A basketball is flying directly at your head! Without even thinking, you reach up and catch the ball before it smashes into your face. How did you do this? Because of a quick reaction time! Reaction time is a measure of your quickness in responding to a stimulus. A reaction occurs when hundreds of thousands of neurons in your brain and nervous system work together to produce a reaction—do you catch, duck, or bat away the ball?

When you spot the ball headed your way, your eyes send visual information to your brain. The brain processes this information and makes a decision about what to do. Then it sends signals to the muscles needed for the reaction. These signals pass through the spinal cord to reach the muscles. Your hands go up and your fingers spread and squeeze—the ball is caught. How fast this happens is your reaction speed. In this activity, you will test your reaction speed.

MOTION NOTION

Over time, you can train your body and brain to work faster and speed up your reaction time. With faster reaction times, you can perform better in many sporting activities.

- **Sit across from your partner.** Hold a ruler at one end so that the other end is just at your partner's index finger. Release the ruler. How fast can your partner grab it? Record the results and repeat the experiment several times. Switch places and have your partner drop the ruler while you try to catch it.

  - What observations did you make?

  - Was there a difference in reaction speed from the first time you or your partner caught the ruler to the last attempt?

  - How did the reaction speed between you and your partner compare?

- **Create a chart or graph to visually present your results.**

> To investigate more, consider that this activity used a visual stimulus (seeing the ruler drop) to trigger a reaction. Design an experiment using the ruler to test your reaction speed using an auditory stimulus instead. Do you observe a difference in reaction speed between the visual and auditory stimulus?

INVOLUNTARY REFLEX

A reflex is not a voluntary decision. Reflexes are involuntary movements. They protect the body and are typically faster than a reaction. One classic reflex is the patellar reflex, a stretch reflex that is triggered by tapping the tendon below your patella (kneecap). This reflex works on a negative feedback circuit.

First, sensory neurons take in information and translate it to an electrical signal that is sent to the CNS. Interneurons in the spinal cord receive the signals and determine how much of a response to the stimulus is needed. They send information to the motor neurons in the muscle fibers to trigger the patellar reflex.

Motor neurons in the quadriceps muscle receive a signal to fire, which causes the muscle to contract. Your lower leg moves up in the air. At the same time, another signal travels to the motor neuron leading to the hamstring muscle on the back of your leg. This signal tells the hamstring to relax so there is no force pulling against the quadriceps muscle as it contracts. This entire loop occurs without involving the brain.

- **Now that you understand how the patellar reflex works, design an experiment to test this reflex yourself.**

  - Does the speed of this reflex vary in different people?

  - Does age or gender affect the reflex speed?

  - Does where you tap the patellar tendon affect the reflex?

  - Can you prevent this reflex from occurring?

- **Compare how long it takes for the reflex to move the lower leg versus a verbal command (reaction) to move the leg.** Is there a difference? Why?

To investigate more, think about what other reflexes are found in all humans. Design an experiment to test these reflexes. What are those reflexes for? How can you benefit from these reflexes? Why do you think these reflexes evolved? Are there any drawbacks to these reflexes?

Chapter Four ▶

Help From
the Organs

DON'T FORGET ABOUT US!

What other organs
have a role in
influencing movement?

The organs in the circulatory system, respiratory system, and the endocrine system all play crucial roles in getting energy to the muscles that need it during movement.

Your muscles and bones might take center stage when your body is moving, but many of your organs contribute to movement behind the scenes. The organs of the circulatory system include the heart, veins, and arteries. This system is also called the cardiovascular system. The organs of the respiratory system include the lungs, bronchi, and diaphragm. The organs of these two systems provide nutrient-rich blood and oxygen to all areas of the body, delivering the fuel that powers movement while also removing waste.

The organs and glands of the endocrine system, including the thyroid and the liver, secrete chemicals that can affect movement. Let's take a look at how these supporting systems help you move!

THE CARDIOVASCULAR SYSTEM

Get ready to start your engines! The cardiovascular system can be seen as the body's engine. It is powered by the most important muscle in your body—the heart!

The heart is the pump that moves blood through the blood vessels throughout your body. Your blood carries necessary oxygen, nutrients, and hormones to all the tissues and organs in your body. It also collects and removes waste products from the cells of the body.

[The heart is made to be an efficient pump.]

Each side of the heart, the left and the right, acts as a separate pump. The two sides are separated by a wall of muscular tissue called the septum. On its right side, the heart receives deoxygenated blood from the body's veins. It pumps the blood into the lungs to receive oxygen. Then the left side of the heart receives the oxygenated blood from the lungs. It pumps blood through the arteries to the organs and tissues throughout the body. Every time your heart beats, both sides of your heart pump.

MOTION NOTION

Only the size of about a closed fist, the heart pumps more than 5 liters of blood throughout your body every minute of the day. It's easily your hardest working muscle!

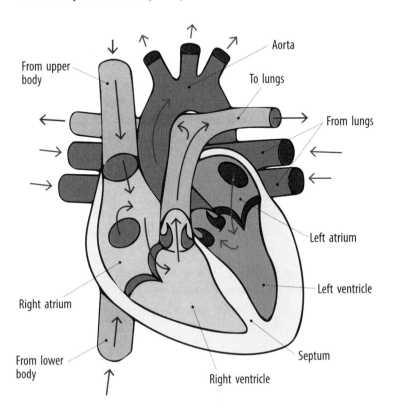

From upper body

Aorta

To lungs

From lungs

Left atrium

Right atrium

Left ventricle

From lower body

Septum

Right ventricle

MOTION NOTION

Have you ever listened to your heart beat? It's the sound of your heart valves closing.

Each side of the heart has two types of chambers. The left atrium and the right atrium are small chambers in the upper half of the heart. They collect blood as it returns to the heart. The ventricles are the larger chambers of the lower half of the heart. They receive blood from each atrium and squeeze to pump the blood out of the heart. In total, there are four heart chambers—two atria and two ventricles.

Heart valves separate the atria and ventricles. They open and close in a coordinated way to keep blood moving in only one direction through the atria to the ventricles. Heart valves also coordinate blood flow to and from the heart.

THE BLOOD VESSEL SUPERHIGHWAY

Once your heart pumps the blood out, the blood vessels deliver it where it needs to go. The body's blood vessels are like superhighways that allow blood to flow quickly and efficiently from the heart to the body's organs and tissues and then back to the heart again. Inside all blood vessels is a hollow area called the lumen. Blood flows through the lumen.

> The size of the blood vessel depends on the amount of blood that moves through it.

Throughout your body, there are three main types of blood vessels: arteries, capillaries, and veins. Arteries carry highly oxygenated blood away from the heart to the body's tissues.

Because the heart pushes blood away from it with great force, arteries must be able to handle high levels of blood pressure. To do so, artery walls are thicker, more elastic, and more muscular than the walls of other blood vessels. Elastic tissue in large artery walls allows them to stretch to handle the blood's pressure and force. Smaller arteries have more muscular walls made of smooth muscle.

The muscles of the artery walls regulate the flow of blood by expanding or contracting. This movement affects the body's blood pressure. When smaller arteries contract so the blood has less room to flow, the pressure of the blood on the artery walls increases.

At the end of arteries, narrower vessels called arterioles carry blood to the capillaries. Because arterioles have to deal with less pressure from the heart, their walls are much thinner than artery walls. Like arteries, arterioles use smooth muscle to regulate blood flow and pressure.

The most common blood vessels in the body are the capillaries. These run through every tissue of the body. They carry blood very close to tissue cells and exchange gases, nutrients, and waste products. The capillaries are the smallest and thinnest blood vessels. Their thin walls allow the gases, nutrients, and waste products to flow in and out more easily while keeping the blood cells inside of the capillaries. Capillaries are connected to arterioles on one side and to venules on the other end.

Once the capillaries have delivered oxygenated blood, veins pick up the deoxygenated blood throughout the body and return it to the heart. Venules start the return process. Connected to the capillaries, they pick up blood and carry it to larger veins.

CHANGING WITH AGE

Age can cause changes to your body's blood vessels. As you get older, blood vessels become less elastic. This leads to an increase in blood pressure, because the heart has to work harder to push the blood through the arteries. A disease called atherosclerosis can cause a buildup of plaque inside the arteries. The plaque is made up of fats, cholesterol, and other substances. It slowly narrows the artery, restricting blood flow. Atherosclerosis is usually the cause of most heart attacks and strokes.

Veins and venules do not face much force from the heart's pumping, so their walls are much thinner, less elastic, and less muscular than artery walls. To push the blood back to the heart, veins use the forces of gravity, inertia, and skeletal muscle contractions. As skeletal muscles contract, they squeeze nearby veins, pushing the blood closer to the heart.

Some veins have one-way valves to prevent blood from flowing backward, away from the heart. When the skeletal muscle relaxes, the valve stops the blood from moving back. When the muscle contracts again, it pushes the blood closer to the heart.

CONTROLLING THE PACE

How do all the cells of the heart muscle squeeze in a coordinated movement? One area of the heart, the sinoatrial node (SA node) controls the action. The SA node is located in the right atrium of the heart. It is similar to a pacemaker. When the atria are filled with blood and the blood begins to flow to the ventricles, the SA node fires. This electrical signal moves through the atria, triggering the atria to contract and push blood into the ventricles.

The signal is briefly delayed at the atrioventricular node (AV node), between the atria and the ventricles. While only a fraction of a second long, this delay gives the atria time to contract without interference from the ventricles. Once the signal passes through the AV node, it moves to the ventricles and triggers them to contract.

Have you ever noticed that your heart beats faster when you exercise? While the SA node sets the pace of your heart rate, the sympathetic and parasympathetic nervous systems can speed or slow your heart rate.

When you are resting, you don't need blood to flow as quickly through your body. During rest periods, the parasympathetic nervous system, which connects to the SA node, slows the heart down.

When you exercise or experience stress, your body needs more oxygen in its muscles. To get the oxygen-rich blood to the muscles quickly, the heart pumps faster. The sympathetic nervous system kicks in. Also connected to the SA node, the sympathetic nervous system causes the heart to pump faster and the heart rate to rise.

When you stop exercising, the parasympathetic nervous system turns on, slowing heart rate again. The sympathetic nervous system also shuts down, reducing heart rate even more.

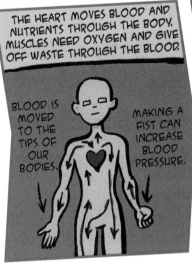

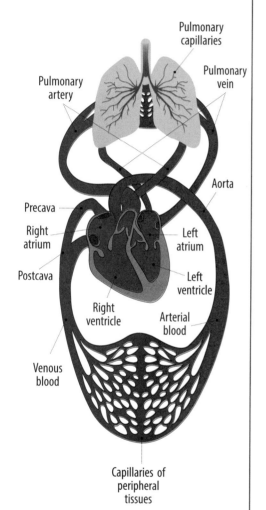

Pulmonary capillaries

Pulmonary vein

Pulmonary artery

Aorta

Precava

Right atrium

Left atrium

Postcava

Left ventricle

Right ventricle

Arterial blood

Venous blood

Capillaries of peripheral tissues

Your resting heart rate is a measure of your heart rate while at rest. Athletes generally have a low resting heart rate. This happens because aerobic exercise trains your heart muscle to be stronger at rest, which lowers the resting heart rate.

THE RESPIRATORY SYSTEM

Your body and muscles need fuel to move. Oxygen is an important part of the body's fuel. While there is plenty of oxygen in the air around you, how does it get into your body, move to your blood, and eventually into your cells?

Simply breathing in air starts a series of processes in your respiratory system that helps your body get all the oxygen it needs.

When you breathe in, you take air into your lungs. The lungs are a pair of large organs found in your chest. Surrounding the lungs, the muscles of respiration work together to push air in and out of the lungs when you inhale.

> Located beneath the lungs, the diaphragm is a muscle that contracts when you breathe in.

When the diaphragm contracts, it creates low pressure in your chest. A gas always moves from an area of high pressure to an area of low pressure. This mechanism allows air and oxygen to travel through your body. The lower pressure in your chest draws air into your lungs. In addition, small intercostal muscles between your ribs also contract and expand your chest, helping the diaphragm.

When you breathe in, air fills the alveoli in your lungs. Alveoli are tiny sacs in the lungs that allow oxygen and carbon dioxide to move between the lungs and blood. Air from the atmosphere has a higher amount of oxygen and lower amount of carbon dioxide than the blood in the capillaries that surround the walls of the alveoli. The gases move from high to low pressure areas through the lining of the alveoli. Oxygen moves from the air into the blood. Carbon dioxide moves from the blood into the air. The blood carries oxygen to the body's tissues, while carbon dioxide releases in the air when you exhale.

When you breathe out, the diaphragm relaxes and the pressure in your lungs increases. The air flows out of the lungs. Contracting the intercostal muscles to pull the chest inward can also send air out of the lungs.

Once oxygen is in your lungs, it must find a way to reach the muscles and other tissues of the body. Gases can exist in both the atmosphere and also in fluid environments, such as the blood. However, the fluid part of blood cannot carry all of the oxygen that the body needs. That's where hemoglobin comes to the rescue!

Hemoglobin is an iron-containing protein within your body's red blood cells. Hemoglobin gives blood its red color. It also carries 99 percent of the oxygen your body needs. The more hemoglobin you have, the more oxygen your blood can carry. Hemoglobin cells pick up oxygen from the lungs. They carry it through the blood and dump it into the muscles and other tissues.

Hemoglobin can pick up, carry, or drop oxygen. What it does depends on three conditions: oxygen pressure, temperature, and pH level.

RESPIRATORY ACIDOSIS

Normally, your lungs remove CO_2 from your blood when you breathe. In some cases, your lungs cannot get rid of enough CO_2. This may happen because of a decreased rate of respiration or a condition such asthma, COPD, pneumonia, or sleep apnea that decreases air movement in the lungs. When too much CO_2 builds up in the blood, it can make your blood too acidic, a condition called respiratory acidosis. The acidity of your blood is measured by its pH. A lower pH means the blood is more acidic, while a higher pH means that it is more basic. Blood normally has a pH between 7.35 and 7.45. If it drops to a pH of 7.35 or lower, a person has acidosis. To treat respiratory acidosis, doctors focus on improving a person's breathing and air movement in their lungs.

In the lungs, hemoglobin finds high oxygen pressure, cooler temperatures, and a basic pH. These conditions cause the hemoglobin to pick up the oxygen from the lungs. It travels through the blood to the muscles. At the muscles, the hemoglobin finds different conditions. A muscle, especially while exercising, has low oxygen pressure, an acidic environment, and a higher temperature. These conditions cause the hemoglobin to drop off its oxygen to the muscles.

After delivering oxygen to the cells, the blood picks up carbon dioxide, a waste product in cells. The blood carries the carbon dioxide back to the lungs, where you exhale it back into the atmosphere.

GETTING OXYGEN FROM THE BLOOD

Your muscles need oxygen to work. Your blood can bring oxygen to the muscles, but if it can't deliver the oxygen effectively, your muscles can't work to their fullest potential.

In the lungs, hemoglobin picks up oxygen. The oxygenated blood flows through the blood vessels into the muscles. The more blood vessels that move through the muscle, the closer oxygen gets to muscle cells. The capillaries have more oxygen than the surrounding muscle tissue. The oxygen flows from the higher pressure area to the lower pressure area and moves from the hemoglobin to the muscle tissues.

In the same way, carbon dioxide flows from the muscle tissue to the blood. The capillaries have less carbon dioxide than the muscle tissue. The hemoglobin picks up a small amount of carbon dioxide from the tissue and carries it back to the lungs.

Most carbon dioxide, however, is carried in the plasma as bicarbonate ion back to the lungs. When some carbon dioxide flows into the red blood cells, the cells convert it into carbonic acid. The carbonic acid molecules separate into bicarbonate ions and hydrogen ions. The hydrogen ions bind to the red blood cells, while the bicarbonate ions move from the red blood cells into the plasma liquid.

When the plasma reaches the lungs, the bicarbonate ions move back into the red blood cells, where they are converted back into carbonic acid and then into carbon dioxide. When you exhale, your lungs expel the carbon dioxide from your body.

BLOOD VESSELS: SUPPLYING THE ACTION

When you exercise, your working muscles need more oxygen to produce energy. Making more energy also produces more carbon dioxide waste that needs to be removed. As a result, your muscles need more blood supply to deliver oxygen and remove carbon dioxide. There isn't enough blood in your body to supply every tissue the maximum amount of blood at the same time. That's why your body can direct blood to the areas that need it the most and limit blood flow to areas that are not active.

When you exercise, the blood vessels in your digestive system and skin receive messages to contract and reduce blood flow—they don't need the oxygen as much as the muscles that are working harder. At the same time, arteries going to the working muscles relax to increase the amount of blood that can flow through, allowing more blood and oxygen to get to the muscle tissue that needs it.

MOTION NOTION

Hemoglobin drops the oxygen it carries faster when temperatures are higher. Therefore, when you exercise and the temperature of your tissues rises, hemoglobin drops its oxygen faster, which helps your working muscles.

The nervous system steps in to control the flow of blood and direct it to where it is most needed. The nervous system sends messages to the muscles in the walls of the blood vessels that regulate blood flow.

Have you ever tried to exercise right after you eat? Not the best idea! After you eat, your digestive system needs blood as it breaks down your food. But your muscles also need blood to work. The two areas are forced to share the blood. As a result, your muscles cannot work as efficiently and your performance suffers. In addition, if your digestive system does not have enough blood flow to do its job, you may find yourself with an upset stomach.

MOTION NOTION

The hypothalamus is a small gland in the brain that assesses the body's environment and releases hormones that control other glands. The hypothalamus coordinates the activities of all other glands in order to keep the body functioning properly.

THE ENDOCRINE SYSTEM

Much like the nervous system, the endocrine system is another control system in the human body. The endocrine system sends chemical messages called hormones that tell different parts of the body what to do.

Several glands in your body produce hormones. These glands are part of the endocrine system and include the hypothalamus, pituitary, thyroid, parathyroid, adrenals, pineal body, and the reproductive glands. Some organs, including the brain, produce and release hormones.

The hypothalamus is responsible for maintaining the body's internal balance, regulating key processes such as heart rate, blood pressure, and body temperature. The pituitary gland releases hormones that control other glands in the body. These glands release hormones that regulate metabolism, development, mood, reproduction, and more. For example, the thyroid gland releases thyroid hormones, which affect the body's metabolism. The pineal gland secretes melatonin, a hormone that regulates sleep patterns. The adrenal glands release several hormones such as cortisol and adrenaline that help you respond to stress.

Endocrine system glands secrete hormones into the blood, where they are carried to tissues and organs throughout the body. These messages tell the tissues to increase or decrease their activity. Hormones only deliver their message to specific tissues or organs that have matching receptor sites. A receptor is a site on a cell that is designed to recognize and accept a specific hormone.

> Only that type of receptor can receive the hormone's message. Otherwise, your bones might get a message meant for your stomach to digest food!

The endocrine and nervous systems work together to initiate and control movement. The nervous system acts quickly by sending signals via nerve impulses to specific glands and muscles. The endocrine system's messages are slower, but have widespread and long-lasting effects. Hormones affect the rate at which cells burn fuels to produce energy needed for movement.

MOTION NOTION

The parathyroid gland secretes parathyroid hormone (PTH), which controls the blood calcium levels and allows the muscular and nervous systems to function optimally. Remember, the muscles need calcium to work.

VOCAB LAB

Write down what you think each of the following words means. What root words can you find for help?

cardiovascular system, **atrium**, **ventricle**, **lumen**, **artery**, **capillary**, **arteriole**, **vein**, **sinoatrial node**, **respiratory system**, **diaphragm**, **hemoglobin**, **external respiration**, **blood doping**, **endocrine system**, **hormone**, and **receptor**.

Compare your definitions with those of your friends or classmates. Did you all come up with the same meanings? Turn to the text and glossary if you need help.

The pituitary gland secretes growth hormone, which stimulates bones and other body tissues to grow. The pancreas produces insulin and glucagon, hormones that work together to maintain a steady level of glucose in the blood. This is the sugar that your body uses for energy.

The hormones adrenaline and noradrenaline, produced in the adrenal glands, help to enhance heart function by increasing your heart rate, constricting blood vessels, and increasing blood pressure. This helps to send blood to active tissues, giving them the energy and oxygen they need.

When you think of human movement, you might not consider organs other than the brain and nervous system as being critical parts of a person's ability to move. But without the respiratory organs, circulatory system, and endocrine system, the muscles and bones wouldn't have the energy they need to move!

There is another source of energy that is needed by the body to move—food! How does the body change the food you eat into energy your muscles can use? Find out in the next chapter.

KEY QUESTIONS

- How do the respiratory system, the circulatory system, and the endocrine system make it possible for the body to move?

- How can you use what you know about each of these systems to help you when you exercise?

HORMONES: THE BODY'S COMMUNICATORS

Hormones are part of your body's communication system—the endocrine system. A hormone is a chemical that carries instructions to specific places in the body. The hormone's message tells your body the action to take, such as make more blood cells, digest food, or grow your bones. Every hormone message has a specific receptor site. This prevents the hormone's message from being delivered to the wrong place. In this activity, you'll design a communication system that demonstrates how the endocrine system ensures that hormones only deliver their message to the right place!

- **Design puzzle pieces that demonstrate the idea that hormones and receptors match to deliver a message to specific sites.** Create matching puzzle pieces for several types of hormones.

- **For each hormone, create instructions for an action that it triggers.**

- **With a group of volunteers, assign half to be hormones and the other half to be receptor sites.** Have them scatter around a room. Give each person a piece of your hormone/receptor puzzle and direct them to find their matches.

  - Which group—hormones or receptors—can move? Which remains stationary?

  - How do the hormone messages get delivered?

  - What happens when the hormone finds the matching receptor site?

> To investigate more, consider what might happen if the wrong hormone is sent to the wrong receptor site. How might that start a chain of mistaken events? Research different diseases that are caused by hormones not working properly.

THE ENDOCRINE SYSTEM: FIGHT OR FLIGHT?

Have you ever been scared suddenly? How did your body react? Your heart probably started beating faster, you may have felt flushed, and you started breathing faster. This happened because of your body's fight-or-flight response. This is an automatic reaction in your body that occurs when you sense a harmful event, attack, or threat. The fight-or-flight response increases your odds of surviving when faced with danger. Your adrenal medulla gland releases hormones such as adrenaline that increase blood pressure, increase heart and breathing rate, turn fat into energy, slow digestion, and dilate the pupils of your eyes. All of these physical changes act to increase your speed and strength. Sometimes, the body activates the flight-or-flight response when it perceives danger, even when no real threat exists. For example, can playing video games trigger the fight-or-flight response in the body?

- **Ask a friend to serve as your test subject.** Before playing a video game, take several measurements, including breathing rate, pulse, and blood pressure. You can get an inexpensive blood pressure cuff at a drugstore. Record each measurement.

- **To measure pain tolerance, poke your friend carefully with a toothpick 10 times while he or she looks away.** Record how many times they can feel the poke. You can also measure and record your friend's reaction time using the activity in Chapter 3 of this book. Record your observations.

- **Have your friend play the action video game for 10 minutes.** Immediately measure their breathing rate and pulse. Resume play for five minutes. Stop to test blood pressure. Resume play for another five minutes. As your friend plays the game, test for pain tolerance. When finished playing, test reaction time again. Record each measurement.

  - How did playing the action video game affect breathing, heart rate, blood pressure, pain tolerance, and reaction time?

  - What if you changed the video game used in the experiment? Does that change your results?

To investigate more, repeat the experiment on more volunteers of different genders and ages. Does gender or age affect the results? Do people who regularly play video games have a different result?

SMOKING

When you smoke, those chemicals cause damage to the tiny hairs that clean your lungs, or cilia. At the same time, smoking causes the cells that produce mucus in the lungs to grow and multiply, which leads to more and thicker mucus. With damaged cilia, the lungs are unable to clean out the mucus. It stays in the lungs, clogs the airways, and causes coughing.

The build-up of excess mucus and other poisonous substances can also lead to lung irritation and damage. Smoking can permanently damage the lungs' air sacs, so less oxygen is carried to your body. These changes increase the risk of lung infection and can cause chronic coughing and wheezing. Some chemicals in cigarette smoke can even cause cells in the lungs to become cancerous.

BREATHE IN, BREATHE OUT

The lungs are the main organ of the respiratory system. They allow us to breathe in the oxygen we need to produce energy for our bodies. Our lungs also exhale waste products, such as carbon dioxide, that are created during energy production. In this activity, you'll build a model of how your lungs work to breathe.

- **First, you need to cut off the bottom of a clear plastic bottle.** You might want to ask an adult for help. Fit the neck of a small balloon over the end of a drinking straw and secure it with a rubber band, being careful not to crush the straw.

- **Insert the straw and balloon into the mouth of the plastic bottle.** Use clay to secure the straw, sealing the mouth of the bottle and allowing a small portion of the straw to stick out of the top. Then fasten a large balloon to the bottom of the bottle with long, strong rubber bands.

  - Which parts of your model represent the mouth, trachea, chest, lung, and diaphragm?

  - What happens to the balloon in the bottle when you pull down on the large balloon? Why does this happen?

  - What happens when you let go of the large balloon? Explain.

> To investigate more, design a model of the lungs and chest cavity that uses two lungs. What other materials will you need? How will you ensure that there is enough space within the chest cavity for both lungs to inflate?

Chapter Five ▶

Fuel to Move

A SANDWICH IS LIKE GASOLINE FOR YOUR BODY!

How does your body get the fuel it needs to move?

Three different processes work to supply your muscles with the fuel they need to be active.

Like any machine, your body needs fuel to move. To drive a car, you need gas. The car's engine uses the stored energy in the gas and converts it to heat and kinetic energy, which is the energy of motion. In your body, the fuel needed for movement comes from the food you eat.

Have you ever heard of athletes eating a special meal before an important game or competition? They are loading their bodies with fuel. When you move, your muscles use the stored chemical energy from the food you've eaten and convert it to heat and kinetic energy.

ADENOSINE TRIPHOSPHATE

Something called adenosine triphosphate (ATP) is the fuel that runs your body. Whether you are sleeping, exercising, or watching television, your body's cells require energy to carry out their jobs. Your body gets the energy it needs from food, by breaking down the food you eat and converting it into high-energy molecules of ATP.

The digestive system breaks down the food you eat into smaller particles that can be absorbed through the intestinal walls. Digestive enzymes attack the proteins, carbohydrates, and fats in your food and reduce them to small, absorbable particles. After they pass through the intestinal wall, some particles are further processed so that they can be safely carried through the blood. The liver breaks down fats into fatty acids. Sugars such as fructose and galactose are converted into glucose. The liver also breaks down proteins into amino acids. The fatty acids, glucose, and amino acids enter the bloodstream, which carries these nutrients to every cell in the body.

Inside the cell, the fatty acids, glucose, and amino acids enter the mitochondria, one of the cell's organelles. An organelle is a structure inside a cell that performs a special function or job. The mitochondria are the energy factories of the cell. This is where most of the work converting oxygen and nutrients into ATP takes place.

How does your body get energy from ATP? By breaking the molecule's strong chemical bonds. If one or two of the bonds holding its phosphate groups are broken, the energy stored in the bonds releases and it can be used to fuel other chemical reactions.

A TINY TANK—STORING ATP

Some ATP is stored in the muscles. When you need energy to move your muscles, your body first turns to its stored ATP. But the tank for stored ATP is very tiny. In fact, your muscles can only store enough ATP to power about two to three seconds of movement. That's not a lot!

WHAT IS ATP?

The ATP molecule is connected to three phosphates by high-energy bonds. These bonds hold the energy your body needs to move and power all of its processes. To get this energy, your body breaks these chemical bonds in a chemical reaction. In your body, enzymes act as catalysts to drive the chemical reaction. An enzyme called ATPase creates a reaction with water to break the bonds in the ATP molecule to release its chemical energy.

> What happens if you want to run a race, play basketball, or dance with your friends? You're going to need a lot more energy than what is stored in your muscles.

METABOLISM

Everything you do requires energy. Your body gets the energy that it needs from a process called metabolism. Metabolism is the series of chemical reactions that occur in the body's cells that provide energy for the body. Metabolism keeps the body functioning and runs even when you are sleeping. Thousands of metabolic reactions happen all the time, keeping the body's cells healthy, fueled, and working.

Once muscle contraction begins, any stores of ATP in the muscles are used up quickly. The muscle needs more ATP right away in order to keep working. Because ATP is so important, the cells in the muscle get to work making more ATP immediately. Several body systems create ATP, either for short bursts of energy or longer sustained movement. Some provide an almost instant supply of ATP, while others make ATP at a slower rate. Some ATP generators get used up very quickly, while others can keep producing ATP forever. **The muscle cells have three primary ways to make ATP.**

- **Phosphocreatine** provides an immediate boost of energy, but lasts only a few seconds.

- **Anaerobic glycolysis** provides energy for activities that need a quick burst of energy for a few minutes.

- **Aerobic respiration** provides a steady stream of energy for activities that do not need a large supply of ATP, but do need it for a long time.

These ATP-making systems work together, providing ATP at different rates and levels as your muscles need it. For example, when you start to move and your muscles contract, your body first uses up the small stores of ATP it has on hand. Then, it turns on all the systems that make ATP. Because these systems work together, they create enough energy for you to perform a series of high kicks or go for a long walk. Your body will have the energy it needs!

PHOSPHOCREATINE: I NEED ATP ASAP!

All muscle cells have a little ATP that they can use immediately. However, that stored ATP only lasts about two to three seconds. So where can your muscles get the ATP they need fast? They can steal it from another source!

Muscle cells also store a high-energy compound called phosphocreatine. Phosphocreatine can be broken down to form ATP. However, it creates only enough fuel for about 10 seconds of high-intensity exercise.

As you sprint in a short race, your muscles quickly break down ATP for energy. As your muscles use ATP, phosphocreatine supplies the energy to make new ATP. But when your muscles use up their stores of phosphocreatine, the supply of ATP to your muscles drops. Without ATP to fuel them, they cannot contract as quickly and powerfully. You slow down. High-intensity activities such as sprinting, swinging a bat, or lifting a heavy weight that last for less than 10 seconds get most of their ATP from phosphocreatine.

ANAEROBIC GLYCOLYSIS

What if instead of running a 100-yard sprint, you are running a 400-meter race? In that case, you need enough ATP to run fast for more than 10 seconds. That's when your body's second ATP-producing system steps up to provide your muscles with energy. Through a process called anaerobic glycolysis, you can make a lot of ATP fast, although not as fast as the phosphocreatine system.

Even though you use ATP to get glucose into the cells, your body ultimately produces double the amount of ATP using that glucose.

Anaerobic glycolysis uses a simple sugar called glucose to form more ATP. Glucose is a molecule with six carbon atoms. A small amount of glucose can be found in your blood. More glucose is stored in your muscles and in your liver as glycogen. Glycogen is like a glucose snowball, with many glucose molecules connected together.

Several chemical reactions have to occur for glycogen to be used for ATP production. In muscles, an enzyme breaks stored glycogen into its glucose pieces. Enzymes in the cells convert glucose and produce ATP.

In the liver, another chemical reaction breaks glycogen into its individual glucose units. The glucose moves into the blood so that it can be transported to the muscle cells that need it. To get the glucose from the blood into the cells, some ATP is required. Once in the cell, enzymes convert the glucose and produce more ATP.

YOUR BODY'S DIGESTIVE SYSTEM WILL TRANSFORM THAT SANDWICH INTO *ATP* MOLECULES.

AND *YOUR* MUSCLES USED A LOT OF ENERGY WHEN YOU RAN THOSE BASES. YOUR BODY KNOWS HOW TO MAKE, STORE, USE, AND REMAKE MORE ENERGY.

HEY! TIME TO MAKE MORE ENERGY, WE NEED IT TO KEEP GOING! WE LOVE IT! THIS FEELS AMAZING! KEEP IT UP!

Anaerobic glycolysis produces energy fairly fast. It creates enough ATP to power heavy activities that typically last for less than three minutes or short bursts of heavy work. Because it doesn't use oxygen to break down the glucose, it is called anaerobic, which means "without oxygen."

> What's the downside of all this quick energy? Anaerobic glycolysis also produces pyruvic acid or pyruvate, a strong acid that quickly causes fatigue.

When fatigue occurs, the muscles stop contracting efficiently. Your muscles can slow the build-up of pyruvic acid with a chemical reaction that uses an enzyme to convert pyruvic acid into lactic acid. However, lactic acid also eventually causes fatigue as it builds in muscles. Even the systems that break down glucose into energy slow down when there is too much acid present.

Luckily, there are a few easy ways to recover from and get rid of lactic acid build-up in your muscles. Getting rid of lactic acid fast is important if you want to get back in the game. You can breathe some of it off. When you breathe, a substance in your blood called bicarbonate combines with lactic acid's hydrogen ions to form a weaker acid called carbonic acid. When the blood passes through the lungs, the carbonic acid converts into carbon dioxide and water. You exhale the carbon dioxide out of your body.

You can also get rid of lactic acid by using your muscles. Doing a cool-down activity, such as walking or other light exercise, helps to get rid of lactic acid because your slow-twitch muscle fibers actually use lactic acid.

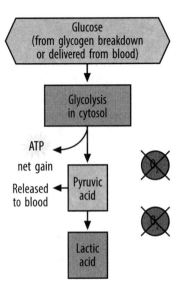

Anaerobic glycolysis and lactic acid formation

Glucose (from glycogen breakdown or delivered from blood)

Glycolysis in cytosol

ATP net gain

Released to blood

Pyruvic acid

Lactic acid

Energy source: glucose

Oxygen use: none

Products: 2 ATP per glucose and lactic acid

Duration of energy provision: 30 to 60 seconds

AEROBIC RESPIRATION: ENERGY FOR THE LONG HAUL

HOW LACTIC ACID CAUSES FATIGUE

The hydrogen ions in lactic acid cause fatigue in muscles. As hydrogen ions build up in the muscle, they compete with calcium ions and block muscle fiber contraction. As a result, the muscle contracts with less force. Hydrogen ions also slow nerve signals to the muscles. This causes uncoordinated signals, which can interfere with motor skills. A runner might find their stride changing as they experience more fatigue. Hydrogen ions can also block an enzyme that is needed for anaerobic glycolysis. When this happens, the muscle has trouble making more ATP. Without ATP, the muscle is forced to slow down.

Sometimes, you need energy for more than a few minutes. Maybe you've signed up to run a 5K race or plan to hike to the top of a mountain. That's when the aerobic respiration system takes over to provide energy for a long time. It provides ATP at a slower rate than the other ATP-producing systems, but can keep fueling the body indefinitely.

Respiration is a process in which food molecules or glucose are turned into ATP. Aerobic respiration uses oxygen to break down glucose for ATP. The glucose comes from several places in the body, including glucose in muscle cells, food in the intestines, glycogen in the liver, and fat reserves in the muscles. In extreme cases, such as during starvation, aerobic respiration uses the body's proteins for glucose to make energy.

> Within the cells, the majority of aerobic respiration takes place in the mitochondria.

The mitochondria have enzymes that break down fats and carbohydrates through a series of chemical reactions. They use oxygen and glucose to create ATP. The only waste products of the process are water and carbon dioxide, which can be breathed out of the body.

Aerobic respiration can be summed up in this equation:

glucose + oxygen → carbon dioxide + water (+ energy)

Aerobic respiration occurs in three stages: glycolysis, the Krebs cycle, and the electron transport chain. Aerobic respiration begins with glycolysis. This is the same process that takes place in anaerobic respiration.

In glycolysis, a series of chemical reactions split glucose molecules into pyruvate molecules. This process produces energy stored in new ATP molecules. It also produces a molecule called nicotinamide adenine dinucleotide hydride (NADH), which carries electrons in the third stage of aerobic respiration, the electron transport chain.

It might sound foolish to use ATP when you are trying to make it, but glycolysis actually creates double the amount of ATP that it uses. So the process ends up with much more ATP than it uses.

Unlike the next two stages of aerobic respiration, glycolysis does not need oxygen. Glycolysis occurs in the cell's cytoplasm, which is the fluid that fills every cell. When glycolysis is complete, the pyruvate and NADH molecules move to the cell's mitochondria for the next stage of aerobic respiration, the Krebs cycle.

In the Krebs cycle, the pyruvate molecules created in glycolysis are converted in a series of chemical reactions that releases electrons and creates hydrogen ions. A hydrogen ion is a hydrogen molecule that has lost its only electron. The hydrogen ions are picked up by other molecules to form flavin adenine dinucleotide hydride ($FADH_2$) molecules and more NADH. Like NADH, $FADH_2$ is an electron carrier in the electron transport chain.

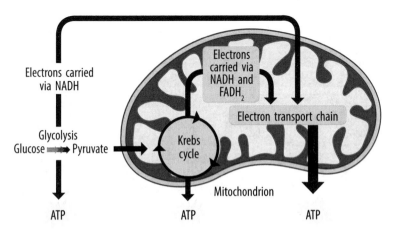

Electrons carried via NADH

Glycolysis
Glucose ⟶ Pyruvate

Electrons carried via NADH and $FADH_2$

Electron transport chain

Krebs cycle

Mitochondrion

ATP   ATP   ATP

You can learn about how ATP is harvested during aerobic respiration in this video.

🔍 electron transport chain animation

MOTION

Some tissues have more mitochondria than others. In the muscles, aerobic muscle fibers have a lot of mitochondria, while anaerobic fibers have fewer mitochondria. Why do you think this is?

The third stage of aerobic respiration, the electron transport system, also takes place in the cell's mitochondria. It uses the hydrogen ions released in the Krebs cycle to produce ATP. The NADH and $FADH_2$ molecules donate the electrons they picked up in the Krebs cycle to make large amounts of ATP.

Aerobic respiration is the slowest of the body's three ATP-producing systems. Even though it starts slowly, it can supply ATP for several hours, as long as the supply of oxygen, carbohydrates, and fats lasts. In aerobic respiration, one molecule of glucose creates a total of 34 ATP molecules. When you walk, jog, hike, and swim, which are all long-duration, low-to-moderate-intensity activities, your body uses aerobic respiration to make the energy you need.

You've learned about what your body has to do to keep moving. In the next chapter, we'll look at what you can do to help your own body stay healthy and able to move the way you want it to!

MANY USES FOR ATP ENERGY

The energy produced during aerobic respiration is used for more than just moving your muscles. It also powers all of your body's systems and processes. It fuels the growth and repair of cells, allows you to build larger molecules, provides energy for chemical reactions throughout your body, keeps your body's temperature constant, and helps your body send messages through the nerves.

KEY QUESTIONS

- Describe and compare the processes of phosphocreatine, anaerobic glycolysis, and aerobic respiration.
- How can you use what you know about how energy is produced in your body to improve your own exercise routines?

NOT ENOUGH FUEL: MUSCLE FATIGUE

Muscles need energy in order to function. Fuel, in the form of ATP, powers your muscles. Have you ever felt your muscles "burn" after strenuous exercise? That's because using a muscle for a long period of time can cause muscle fatigue. When muscles become fatigued, they cannot work as efficiently. In addition, waste products from using fuel to power muscle movement builds up in the muscles, which can lead to more muscle fatigue. Let's see what that feels like!

- **Loop a rubber band around your thumb and your ring finger.** Stretch your ring finger so that you feel tension in the rubber band. You might want to mark a piece of paper with the positions of your thumb and finger so that you keep the stretch constant. Have someone time how long you can hold this position.

  - What muscles are you using in this activity?

  - What do you notice about these muscles during the activity? How do they feel? Explain.

- **Repeat the experiment using different fingers.** What do you observe?

To investigate more, repeat this activity daily for at least two weeks. Does the amount of time you can hold the stretch change? Why? What is happening to the muscles? What other muscles can you test for muscle fatigue? Do you get a different outcome with different muscles?

VOCAB LAB

Write down what you think each of the following words means. What root words can you find for help?

ATP, mitochondria, phosphocreatine, anaerobic glycolysis, aerobic respiration, glycogen, pyruvate, Krebs cycle, and **electron transport chain**.

Compare your definitions with those of your friends or classmates. Did you all come up with the same meanings? Turn to the text and glossary if you need help.

EXTRACTING ENERGY FROM SUGAR

The cells in your body use sugar molecules to make energy. They can break down larger carbohydrate molecules into simple sugars, which are then used to make energy. Yeast, a single-celled fungus, also makes energy from sugar molecules. In the presence of oxygen, yeast breaks down sugar molecules to produce energy, along with carbon dioxide and water. In this activity, you'll feed sugar to yeast and observe the by-products of energy production.

Ideas for Supplies ▼

- small clear plastic soda bottle
- warm water
- packet of yeast
- sugar
- small balloon

MOTION**N**OTION

When no oxygen is present, yeast uses a process called fermentation to extract energy from the sugar molecules. Fermentation produces less energy than sugar metabolism with oxygen.

- **First, pour about 1 inch of warm water into a clean, clear plastic bottle.** Empty a yeast packet into the bottle and gently swirl it to dissolve the yeast. As the yeast dissolves, it becomes active and begins to react with its environment.

WOOHOO! GO *YEAST*, GO!

- **To feed the yeast, add some sugar.** Place a stretched balloon over the neck of the bottle. Let the bottle sit in a warm place for about 20 minutes. What happens?

- **Because yeast is microscopic fungi, you can't actually see the yeast processing the sugar into energy with the naked eye.** However, you can observe the by-products of the process.

  - What by-products are formed when the yeast makes energy from sugar?

  - How can you tell?

- **Try varying the conditions in the activity, such as room temperature, size of container, water temperature, and the amount of sugar.** Does changing these conditions affect the amount of by-product created by the yeast?

To investigate more, consider what might happen if you feed different types of sugar to yeast, such as white sugar, brown sugar, syrup, and honey. Which causes the yeast to create the most gas? Why do you think this occurs?

NOT ALL SUGAR IS THE SAME

Not all sugar is the same—sugar can be natural or refined. Natural sugars are found in fruit as fructose or in dairy products as lactose. In addition to vitamins and minerals, fruits have fiber, which slows down the digestion process, helping prevent increases in blood sugar and fat storage. Refined sugars are processed from sugar cane or sugar beets into sucrose or fructose. These sugars sweeten cakes, cookies, and other foods. Food manufacturers add high-fructose corn syrup to many processed foods. In the body, refined sugars are quickly broken down into glucose, which causes spikes in insulin and blood sugar levels, while fructose is metabolized in the liver and increases fat cell production.

Ideas for Supplies ▼

- two cans, one smaller and one larger
- pencil
- cork
- needle
- thermometer
- different kinds of food
- matches

HOW MUCH CHEMICAL ENERGY IS IN YOUR FOOD?

Food supplies your body with chemical energy to power all of its processes and movement. Some foods contain more energy than others. In this activity, you will build a calorimeter to measure the heat energy released by burning a food item. Using this method, you will be able to compare the energy in different types of food.

CAUTION: This activity involves matches and burning food, so supervision by an adult is necessary.

- **Using a can opener, remove the top and bottom from the large can.** Drill or punch a few holes along the bottom of the large can so that air is able to pass through the can. You may want to ask an adult for help.

- **Remove the top of the smaller can and drill or punch two holes opposite each other about 1 inch from the top.** Slide a pencil through the two holes.

- **Next, carefully push the dull end of a needle into a cork.** The sharp end should stick up so that you can use it to hold the food you will test.

- **Stand the cork on a flat, non-flammable surface.** Put the large can over it. Then place the smaller can into the large one, using the pencil as a support to hang it over the cork and needle. Make sure that there is enough space between the bottom of the small can and the needle and make adjustments if necessary. Remove both cans for a minute so you can access needle.

- **Select several small pieces of food to test, such as different types of nuts, marshmallows, gummy bears, and pretzels.** Which items of food do you think have the most energy? Place the first food to be tested on the needle.

- **To begin the experiment, fill the small can about half-full with water.** Then measure the temperature of the water in the small can and record it. Put the cork on the non-flammable surface and light the food on fire. Quickly place the large can over the cork and hang the small can with water above the flame.

- **Allow the food to burn until it burns out.** Then, carefully remove the small can by holding the ends of the pencil, and put it on a flat, heat-proof surface. Stir the water and measure its temperature. Repeat this procedure to test the other food items. Make sure to handle the hot food carefully.

- **Record your observations.**

  - What happened to the water temperature when you burned the food?

  - Which items of food caused the temperature to increase the most? Which caused less change in temperature?

  - Do you think your calorimeter captures all of the energy released by burning food? Why or why not?

  - Based on your results, what types of food should you eat when your body needs energy?

- **Create a chart or graph to visually present your results.**

To investigate more, test and compare foods containing natural sugars vs. foods with refined sugars. What do you note about your results? How do you explain your results?

Chapter Six ▶

Moving On

How does diet and exercise affect your body and movement?

Getting the right amount of exercise and eating healthy food are crucial to keeping your body healthy and fit!

Your body is a finely tuned, complex machine. You perform your best when all of the systems involved in movement, from your skeletal system to your nervous system, are functioning at optimal levels. Diet and exercise play key roles in keeping your body healthy and moving well.

Regular movement can reduce blood pressure and lead to a stronger heart, as well as increase bone density and improve blood cholesterol levels. Movement also strengthens the immune system, reduces the risk of cancer and heart disease, and even reduces stress, anxiety, and depression. So don't waste any more time—get up and get moving!

EFFECTS OF INACTIVITY

Physical inactivity affects your body inside and out. A lack of exercise can make your muscles weak and make it more difficult to maintain a healthy weight. Your bones will not be as strong as they could be.

But did you know that inactivity can also affect your internal organs? All of your organ systems, including your cardiovascular system, nervous system, and gastrointestinal system, suffer when you don't move enough.

If you aren't using some of your muscles regularly, your body soon decides that these muscles are not that important. The muscles start to break down in a process called muscle atrophy. As your muscles atrophy, they get weaker, which makes it harder to finish everyday activities.

Throughout your lifetime, your bones are constantly being broken down and rebuilt. Getting rid of old bone cells and replacing them with new cells helps keep your bones as strong as possible. But if you aren't active and using your bones to move and support your body's weight, the old cells are broken down faster than new ones are generated. This causes your bones to become weak, brittle, and more likely to break.

Physical inactivity also affects your cardiovascular system. Your heart is the most important muscle in your body. Like all other muscles, if you don't exercise and use it, the heart begins to atrophy. A weakened heart has more difficulty pumping oxygen to your cells, making you feel more tired. Physical inactivity can make your blood vessels become thicker and less flexible. At the same time, the blood flowing through them becomes stickier. Together, this increases the risk of a blood clot, which is a mass of blood cells that can block the blood vessel.

> Blood clots can be very serious and in some cases can lead to a heart attack or stroke.

HEART ATTACK OR STROKE?

A blood clot can cause either a heart attack or a stroke. A heart attack occurs when a blood clot blocks blood flow to the heart. The heart muscle does not receive enough oxygenated blood and begins to die. When a blood clot blocks the arteries that supply blood to the brain, a stroke occurs. The blockage in the blood vessel cuts off blood flow and oxygen to the brain, which disrupts the brain's functioning and the brain cells begin to die.

Lack of exercise can also impact your endocrine system, which regulates hormones. Insulin is a hormone that controls the amount of sugar in your blood. It helps cells absorb sugar from the blood and use it for energy. Insulin binds to a receptor on a muscle cell, which allows the cell to use sugar for energy.

When a person is physically inactive, their muscle cells do not use insulin as much. This can lead to the binding sites for insulin to start to disappear. This causes the body to become less responsive to insulin and can even lead to Type 2 diabetes if the body stops responding to insulin completely.

[
Physical inactivity can also cause your brain and nervous system to function at a lower level.
]

Inactivity has been linked to cognitive decline and dementia in the elderly. It has been linked to depression and anxiety. When you exercise, your brain releases hormones called endorphins that dull pain. Endorphins also lead to feelings of happiness. A lack of endorphins means a risk of developing depression or anxiety.

Your immune system is your defense against germs and illness. White blood cells and antibodies carried in your blood fight off bacteria and viruses. Because physical inactivity leads to a weaker heart muscle, the body cannot pump blood as efficiently. This makes it harder for the infection-fighting white blood cells and antibodies to reach sites of infection and defend the body against disease.

Your gastrointestinal system digests food and excretes waste from your body. Muscles line the digestive tract to help your body digest food. Physical inactivity can make these muscles less efficient, leading to slower digestion and elimination of waste.

EXERCISE TO BUILD BONES

A healthy body begins with strong bones. Even though most of your bone is formed during childhood and adolescence, your bones continue to be broken down and remade as an adult. And you can use exercise to build denser, stronger bones.

When compression forces squeeze bones together, bones react by growing stronger. The combination of gravity and your body weight helps to build stronger bones. Every step you take puts your spinal column under a compressive load. This load triggers bone growth.

Weight-bearing exercise, such as walking and running, builds up the bones in your legs and torso. Lifting weights can also stimulate bone growth. The weight places a compressive load on the bones, causing them to grow.

STRENGTHENING MUSCLE

Muscles are always changing. If you don't use them, they begin to atrophy and grow smaller and weaker. However, if you train your muscles, they can get stronger and faster.

Having more muscle mass and stronger muscles can help you in many ways. It makes it easier to do all of your daily activities without getting tired. You can participate in many different sport activities and injuries are less frequent. And because muscles use a lot of energy, they burn more calories, which can help you maintain a healthy weight.

MOTION NOTION

As you get older, your bones can lose strength. But with physical activity, you can reduce the effects of aging on your bones. Walking, running, and lifting weights can all promote bone growth and help you keep your bones strong as you age. As a teenager, it might seem as though you have plenty of time to build up your bones, but establishing a habit of exercise early in your life is the easiest way to keep exercising later in life!

At the 2016 Rio de Janeiro Summer Olympic Games, the weightlifting gold medalist in the men's +105kg category, Lasha Talakhadze of Georgia, completed a lift of 568 pounds.

Muscles grow when put under stress, causing them to adapt. Strength training is one way to put muscles under stress so that they will grow stronger. Weights that muscles can lift without stress will do little to improve strength. Instead, the goal is to push muscles enough to cause stress without causing injury.

When you lift the weight the first time, only some of the muscle fibers are called to action. As lifting continues, the working fibers become fatigued and the muscle recruits more fibers to lift the weight. The process of used fibers getting fatigued and new fibers being called into action continues until all the muscle fibers are used and fatigued. At that point, the muscle has been adequately worked.

> Over time, muscle will adapt to a load.
> So if you keep training the same way
> or lifting the same amount of weight,
> your muscles will stop getting stronger.

You might begin to notice that you can easily finish more than 20 repetitions of an exercise without your muscles getting fatigued. To avoid hitting an exercise plateau, you can progressively increase the load as the muscle adapts.

The amount of the load increase varies by person and also by the size of the muscle. Typically, a 10-percent increase in load is adequate.

HOW THE BODY ADAPTS TO STRENGTH TRAINING

When you do strength training, several changes occur in your body, both in your muscles and in your nervous system. After about eight to 12 weeks of regular strength training, the muscles might increase in size. This is called hypertrophy. This increase occurs in both the slow-twitch and fast-twitch muscle fibers.

The muscles also experience an increase in actin and myosin, the proteins that trigger muscle contraction. Having more of these proteins increases the muscle's pulling power, making it stronger.

Strength training also affects the brain and nervous system. Within four to eight weeks of regular strength training, these changes can increase muscle strength without changing the size of the muscle's fibers. With regular training, the body is able to recruit more muscle fibers into action. It also increases the frequency of the brain's signals for contraction. As the muscles receive these signals more often, they spend more time contracting than they do relaxing. Training also coordinates the motor units so that all the muscle fibers pull at the same time, which generates the most force.

STRONG BODY, STRONG MIND

In addition to strengthening your body, exercise might actually help you develop a strong mind. Scientists are learning that exercise can help you learn, remember, and process information.

MOTION NOTION

Strength training can increase the threshold for the Golgi tendon activation. More force is needed to trigger the reflex, allowing the muscle to generate more force before the reflex stops it.

MUSCLE RECOVERY

Did you know that muscle growth actually occurs after a workout, not during? Muscles grow during the recovery time between workouts. That's why many people who strength train their muscles do not work the same muscles on consecutive days. They are giving their fatigued muscles time to recover and grow. In contrast, lifting weights every day stresses the muscle too often. This interferes with the recovery process and leads to reduced performance.

Muscles need protein to add structure to the muscle and carbohydrates to fuel muscle building. They also need time for recovery and adaptation to occur. So eating enough of these two nutrients after a heavy workout is important to make sure your muscles recover properly and grow stronger.

Exercise might even make you smarter. For many years, scientists believed dead brain cells could not be replaced as a person ages. However, some studies have shown regular aerobic exercise may add new brain cells.

[
Exercise may increase the size of certain brain regions, including the hippocampus and the prefrontal cortex.
]

Scientists believe that aerobic exercise might improve memory and thinking by stimulating chemicals in the brain that affect the health of brain cells, the growth of new blood vessels in the brain, and the number and survival of new brain cells. So exercising for a strong body can help you produce more brain cells.

As we age, our brains slow down and brain cells die. For some people, this process occurs more quickly than it does for others. They might lose the ability to remember, pay attention, and make decisions. For some, they may even lose the ability to speak. These changes are a condition called dementia.

Alzheimer's disease is one form of dementia. For patients with Alzheimer's, abnormal clumping and tangling of nerve cells in the brain's hippocampus impair the ability to think or remember things. The connections between brain cells break down, so that the cells stop sending messages and sometimes die.

Scientists are currently investigating the effects of exercise on Alzheimer's disease. They hope that exercise may be able to replace some of the dead or damaged cells in the brain's hippocampus, which may be able to stop or slow the effects of the disease.

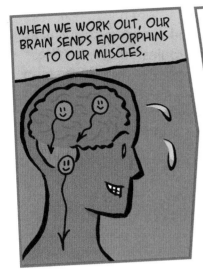

EXERCISE FOR MOOD AND MIND

Have you ever noticed that you're in a better mood right after you exercise? That's because exercise is the body's way to naturally enhance mood. Many studies have found that regular exercise can improve the way people think and feel about themselves. Exercise has been shown to reduce feelings of anxiety and stress. It can also minimize the negative symptoms of depression.

[
The link between mood and depression are not entirely known, but physical activity can definitely ease symptoms of anxiety or depression and generally make you feel good.
]

MOTION NOTION

The hippocampus is a small area of the brain that is responsible for memory and emotion.

Scientists believe that regular physical activity can improve mood in several ways. When you exercise, your brain releases feel-good chemicals such as neurotransmitters and endorphins that can ease depression symptoms and improve mood. Exercise can also reduce immune system chemicals that worsen depression. By increasing body temperature, movement might have a calming effect on mood.

Regular exercise can help a person gain confidence and feel better about themselves and their appearance. It can take your mind off worries and help break the cycle of negative thoughts frequently found in anxiety and depression. Exercise can also help a person increase their interactions with other people, giving them more opportunities to meet and socialize with others.

TOO MUCH OF A GOOD THING

Regular exercise has many benefits for the body and mind. But sometimes, too much exercise can be bad for you. For a small number of people, exercise can become an unhealthy obsession. Putting too much emphasis on exercise, at the expense of other areas of your life, is cause for concern.

There are other issues to consider when starting an exercise program. Very intense or extremely long exercise sessions can lead to serious health issues. Sometimes, even moderate physical activity can cause problems, especially if a person has an underlying health condition or is exercising in extreme conditions. While regular exercise can strengthen the heart, people with heart disease or structural heart defects may experience sudden cardiac arrest while exercising. For people with asthma, exercise can worsen their conditions.

Some people will experience some sort of exercise-related injury. Acute injuries called macro-traumas happen fast, but cause a lot of a pain. Common acute injuries include broken bones, sprains, pulled muscles, torn ligaments, and concussions.

[
Micro-trauma injuries, also called overuse injuries, result from frequent, repeated overuse of muscles, tendons, ligaments, joints, and bones.
]

A tiny rip or tear might be barely noticeable at first. You might feel a bit sore after physical activity, but there is nothing that seems particularly concerning. During weeks or months, hundreds or thousands of repetitions of the same movements causing soreness or discomfort can take their toll on your body.

Examples of this type of overuse injury include tendonitis, which is an inflammation of a tendon. Shin splints are caused by repeated trauma to connective tissues that attach muscles to the shin bone, while a stress fracture is a tiny crack in a bone. Without rest, these chronic injuries cause pain and interfere with movement. An overuse injury might cause so much discomfort that you have trouble walking, lifting your arms over your head, or bending your knees.

Exercise in extreme conditions, both cold and hot, can also do more harm than good. In cold temperatures, exercising for long periods can lead to several types of injury. Your body temperature can drop to dangerously low levels, around 95 degrees Fahrenheit (35 degrees Celsius), a serious condition called hypothermia.

MOTION NOTION

To help treat many overuse injuries, such as a strained tendon, the RICE treatment is recommended. RICE stands for Rest, Ice, Compression, and Elevation.

EXERCISE AND BETTER SLEEP

Have you ever noticed that after a day of exercise, you often sleep better at night? This happens because exercise improves your body's circadian rhythm. A circadian rhythm is the body's natural cycle of sleep and being awake. Exercise raises the body's daytime temperature. This triggers the release of hormones that make you sleepy. When inactive, the body has a lower daytime temperature. This disrupts the release of sleep hormones, making it harder to get a good night's sleep.

In extreme cold, your extremities, such as your fingers, toes, and the tip of your nose, can freeze. When the internal temperature of the body drops too low, your body diverts blood to support life-sustaining functions. Blood vessels in the extremities narrow. Without enough warm blood, the skin tissue in these areas begins to freeze and die. You have frostbite.

Exercising in extreme heat can also cause serious harm. Some heat-related injuries, such as heat cramps, are mild, while others, such as heat stroke, are severe and can be life-threatening. If you are working hard in hot, humid conditions, you are at risk of developing a heat injury.

While it's true that injury can happen during exercise, this just means that you have to be careful. Listen to your body. Exercise is one of the best things you can do for your body, along with getting the nutrients and sleep you need to keep your body and your brain healthy. The body you're born with is the only one you'll have for your entire life—keep it working as well as possible so you can enjoy the world on your own terms. Happy moving!

KEY QUESTIONS

- What are some of the risks involved with exercise? How can you make sure to avoid getting injured?
- Why is it important to vary your exercise routines?
- What are some things you can do to motivate yourself to exercise even on days you don't feel like it?

THE EFFECT OF EXERCISE ON THE BRAIN

Scientists believe that regular exercise is an important part of keeping the brain healthy and working well. Exercise may stimulate nerve cells to produce chemicals that encourage brain cells to grow and connect with other brain cells. Being active can help a person focus better, make decisions faster, and even heal faster from a brain injury. Activity might also reduce the risk of dementia as a person ages. In this activity, you will design an experiment to test the effect of exercise on the brain.

- **To begin, develop a memory test and give it to a group of volunteers.** Record their results. Once they have finished, divide your volunteers into two groups—one that performs an aerobic activity before the memory test and one that performs a sedentary activity before the test.

- **Have one group do 10 minutes of an aerobic activity and the other do 10 minutes of a sedentary activity.** After they perform their activity, give them a second memory test. Record your observations and results.

  - What did you observe?

  - Did the scores change or stay the same before and after each person's assigned activity?

  - Did the group that exercised aerobically show any effect on their memory test scores?

- **Make a table or graph to present your results.**

VOCAB LAB

Write down what you think each of the following words means. What root words can you find for help?

atrophy, endorphins, adapt, strength training, dementia, macro-trauma, micro-trauma, frostbite, and **heat stroke**.

Compare your definitions with those of your friends or classmates. Did you all come up with the same meanings? Turn to the text and glossary if you need help.

To investigate more, consider whether more exercise or a different type of exercise would have a greater impact on memory. Design an experiment to find out.

THE EFFECT OF EXERCISE ON LUNG CAPACITY

Lung capacity is the amount of air that you can fit into your lungs. When you perform aerobic exercise, such as running or biking, you breathe deeper and more often to increase the amount of air and oxygen going into your lungs. Does a person's lung capacity increase with regular aerobic exercise? In this activity, you'll design an experiment to find out.

- **One way to measure a person's lung capacity is to use a machine called a spirometer.** You can also measure lung capacity with a balloon. Stretch out the balloon several times to make sure it is not too stiff. Take the deepest breath you can. Then exhale all of the air in your lungs into the balloon. Pinch the balloon shut and tie it to prevent any air from escaping. Measure the diameter of the balloon and record your results. This measures your vital capacity, the largest amount of air that can be exhaled after taking a deep breath. Repeat several times, recording each measurement.

- **Perform an aerobic activity for at least 10 minutes.** After you finish, measure your lung capacity again. Record your measurements. Did you observe any short-term changes in lung capacity after aerobic exercise?

- **Compare your results to another person.**

  - Are they similar or different?

  - Why do you think people have different lung capacities?

- **To test the long-term effect of aerobic exercise on lung capacity, design and follow an aerobic workout routine for four weeks.** At the end of each week, re-measure your lung capacity.

  - Do you observe any changes in lung capacity? Explain.

  - What difference do you notice week to week?

  - Do you think one week is long enough to change lung capacity? Explain.

To investigate more, consider that musicians who blow into instruments such as the clarinet or trumpet need to have a lot of air in their lungs. Does playing this type of instrument over time help them develop a larger lung capacity? Design an experiment to find out.

GLOSSARY

abduction: the process of changing the rate of speed of an object's movement.

acceleration: the process of increasing the speed of an object's movement.

actin: a protein that combines to form the thin filament of the muscle fiber.

action potential: a brief pulse of electrical current that is generated by a neuron.

adapt: to make a change to become better suited to environment.

adduction: movement toward the body.

adenine: a compound that is one of the four bases of nucleic acids that is used to build DNA.

adenosine triphosphate: a nucleotide that is the primary source of energy in all living cells.

adrenal glands: endocrine glands that produce a variety of hormones, including adrenaline and cortisol.

adrenaline: a hormone secreted by the adrenal glands that increases rates of blood circulation, breathing, and carbohydrate metabolism and prepares muscles for exertion.

aerobic respiration: the process that uses oxygen to break down food and turn it into energy.

aerobic: exercise that results in the body circulating more oxygen.

agonist: a muscle that activates and produces the force necessary for movement.

alveoli: the tiny air sacs in the lungs where the exchange of oxygen and carbon dioxide takes place.

Alzheimer's disease: a form of dementia that grows worse over time and affects memory, thinking, and behavior.

amino acid: an organic compound that serves as a building block for proteins.

anaerobic glycolysis: production of energy without oxygen.

anaerobic: without oxygen.

anatomy: the branch of science concerned with the bodily structure of humans, animals, and other living organisms.

angular motion: when an object moves around an axis of rotation.

antagonist: a muscle that relaxes to produce force in the opposite direction of an agonist muscle.

anterior: located near the front.

antibodies: large, Y-shaped proteins that are recruited by the immune system to identify and neutralize foreign objects such as bacteria and viruses.

appendicular skeleton: the parts of the skeleton that attach to the axial skeleton, including the arms, legs, scapula, clavicle, and pelvis.

arteriole: the tiny blood vessel that connects arteries to capillaries.

artery: a blood vessel that carries blood away from the heart to the body.

asthma: a respiratory condition marked by spasms in the bronchi of the lungs, causing difficulty in breathing.

astronomer: a person who studies the planets and stars.

ATP: the fuel that runs your body. Short for adenosine triphosphate, ATP is a molecule with strong bonds holding three phospate groups that, when broken, release energy.

ATPase: an enzyme that creates a reaction with water to break the bonds in the ATP molecule to release its chemical energy.

atrioventricular node: the electrical relay station between the upper and lower chambers of the heart.

atrium: one of the two upper chambers of the heart. Plural is atria.

atrophy: a loss of muscle mass.

autonomic nervous system: the part of the nervous system that controls unconscious actions, such as breathing and heart beating.

axial skeleton: the central part of the skeleton consisting of the skull, vertebrae, ribs, and sternum.

axis: an imaginary line about which a body rotates.

axon: the long threadlike part of a nerve cell along which impulses are conducted from the cell body to other cells.

bacteria: microscopic, one-celled organisms.

balance: an even distribution of weight enabling someone or something to remain upright and steady.

ball-and-socket joint: a joint where a ball-like end of one bone fits into a curved depression in another bone, such as the hip joint, allowing movement in all directions.

basal ganglia: a group of structures in the base of the brain involved in coordination of movement.

BCE: put after a date, BCE stands for Before Common Era and counts down to zero. CE stands for Common Era and counts up from zero. These non-religious terms correspond to BC and AD. This book was printed in 2017 CE.

bending: when a compression force acts on one side of an object and a tension force acts on the other side.

bicarbonate ion: a negatively charged molecule consisting of one carbon, three oxygen, and one hydrogen atom.

binding site: a region on a protein or piece of DNA or RNA to which specific molecules and/or ions may form a chemical bond.

biomechanics: the application of the principles of mechanics to the study of biological systems.

biomechanist: a scientist who studies biomechanics.

blood clot: a mass of blood that becomes gel-like.

blood doping: an illegal method of improving athletic performance by artificially boosting the blood's ability to bring more oxygen to muscles.

blood pressure: the pressure of the blood against the inner walls of the blood vessels.

blood vessel: a tubular structure that carries blood through the tissues and organs, such as a vein, artery, or capillary.

bone: a rigid organ that is part of the skeleton.

bone density: the amount of bone mineral in a bone.

bone marrow: the fatty tissue inside bone cavities that makes red and white blood cells.

brain stem: the base of the brain that is connected to the spinal cord and controls the flow of messages between the brain and the rest of the body.

brittle: hard but likely to break or shatter easily.

buoyancy: the ability to float in water or air or some other fluid.

bursa: a fluid-filled sac or saclike cavity, especially at a joint.

calcium: a mineral found mainly in the hard part of bone.

calcium carbonate: a mineral that adds strength and hardness to bone.

calcium phosphate: a mineral that adds strength and hardness to bone.

callosum: tissue that connects the two cerebral hemispheres.

calorimeter: a device that measures the heat energy in food.

cancellous bone: the spongy tissue that makes up the inside of bone.

capillaries: tiny blood vessels that connect the smallest arteries with the smallest veins and deliver oxygen and nutrients to the body's tissues.

carbohydrates: an important source of energy found in the sugars, starches, and fibers in fruits, grains, vegetables, and milk products.

carbon dioxide: a colorless, odorless, gas, CO_2, present in the atmosphere and formed during respiration.

cardiac arrest: a heart attack.

cardiac muscle: muscle tissue found in the heart.

cardiovascular system: the body system that includes the heart and blood vessels. Also called the circulatory system.

cartilage: a tough, fibrous connective tissue.

catalyst: an enzyme that increases the rate of a chemical reaction.

cell: the basic building block of all living organisms.

central nervous system: the brain and spinal cord.

cerebellum: the part of the brain at the back of the skull that coordinates and regulates muscular activity.

cerebral cortex: the outer layer of the cerebrum.

cerebrum: the major part of the brain, where most higher-level functions and processing occur.

chemical reaction: the process when two or more molecules interact and change.

cholesterol: a waxy, fat-like substance that is found in all cells of the body.

chronic: recurring.

circulation: the movement of a fluid in a closed system.

circulatory system: the body system that includes the heart and blood vessels. Also called the cardiovascular system.

circumferential: at or near the boundary line of an object.

cognitive: conscious and unconscious brain processes, such as perceiving, thinking, learning, and remembering information.

collagen: a protein that provides a soft framework for bone.

compound: a substance made up of two or more elements.

compression: a pushing or squeezing force.

concentric: a contraction that shortens a muscle.

connective tissue: the tendons, ligaments, and joint capsules that connect bones with bones and muscles with bones to provide support for the skeleton and allow it to move.

contractility: the ability of a muscle to create tension to move.

contraction: when muscle fibers shorten and produce a force.

coordination: the ability to use different parts of the body together smoothly and efficiently.

coronary: relating to the arteries that are around the heart and supply it with blood.

cortex: the outer layer of the cerebrum.

cortical bone: the hard outer layer of bone.

curvilinear: contained by or consisting of a curved line or lines.

cytoplasm: the jelly-like fluid inside a cell.

dementia: a group of brain diseases that cause the gradual decline in a person's ability to think and remember.

dendrite: a short, branched extension of a nerve cell along which impulses received from other cells are transmitted to the cell body.

deoxygenated: without oxygen.

depression: a serious medical condition in which a person feels very sad and hopeless and often is unable to live in a normal way.

diaphragm: the muscle that separates the chest from the abdomen.

digestive system: the body system that breaks down food, absorbs nutrients, and filters waste.

dopamine: a neurotransmitter.

eccentric: a contraction when the muscle resists lengthening.

effort: the force applied in a lever system.

elasticity: the ability of a muscle to return to its normal resting length after being stretched.

electron transport chain: part of the aerobic respiration process in which ATP is produced.

endocrine system: a group of glands that produce hormones that regulate many processes in the body, including growth and metabolism.

endorphins: a group of hormones released in the brain that reduce feelings of pain and improve mood.

endurance: when talking about muscles, the amount of time a muscle can maintain a contraction.

energy system: a system that generates the ability to do things, to work.

engineer: to design or build a machine or structure.

enzyme: a protein that speeds up a chemical reaction.

excitability: the size of a response to an input signal.

excitatory: something that triggers an increase in a neuron's firing.

extensibility: the ability of a muscle to stretch beyond its normal length.

extension: movement that increases the angle between two bones.

external respiration: the exchange of gases between the atmosphere and the lungs in humans.

fascicle: a bundle of muscle fibers.

fatigue: impairment of muscle performance.

fatty acids: a carboxylic acid with a long aliphatic chain, which is either saturated or unsaturated.

feedback loop: the path by which some of the output of a circuit, system, or device is returned to the input.

fight-or-flight response: the brain's response to defend itself against or flee from a perceived threat.

flat bone: a type of bone that is flat and functions to protect internal organs and provide an attachment site for muscles.

flavin adenine dinucleotide hydride (FADH): an electron carrier in the electron transport chain stage of aerobic respiration.

flexibility: the range of motion around a joint.

flexion: movement that decreases the angle between two bones.

force: a push or pull upon an object resulting from the object's interaction with another object. When talking about muscles, force is the maximum contraction strength of a muscle.

friction: the force resisting the motion of two objects sliding against each other.

frostbite: an injury caused by freezing of the skin and underlying tissues.

fructose: a simple sugar found in honey, many fruits, and some vegetables.

fulcrum: the point on which a lever rests or is supported and on which it pivots.

fungus: any member of the kingdom of living things, such as mushrooms, molds, and rusts, that have no chlorophyll and must live in or on plants, animals, or decaying material.

galactose: a simple sugar often formed from lactose.

gastrointestinal: relating to the digestive system.

gland: an organ in the human body that secretes particular chemical substances for use in the body.

glucagon: a hormone formed in the pancreas that promotes the breakdown of glycogen to glucose in the liver.

glucose: a sugar that is the major source of energy for cells.

glycogen: a form of glucose with several glucose molecules stuck together.

glycolysis: the breakdown of glucose by enzymes, releasing energy and pyruvic acid.

Golgi tendon reflex: an automatic action in which a muscle contraction causes the agonist muscle to lengthen and relax.

Golgi tendon: a proprioceptive sensory receptor organ that senses changes in muscle tension.

gravity: the force of attraction between an object and a planet (the earth).

heat stroke: a serious medical emergency that can occur when the body is exposed to excessive hot temperatures.

hemispheres: either of the two halves of the brain.

hemoglobin: the protein in red blood cells that combines with oxygen.

hinge joint: a joint that permits movement in only one direction, such as the elbow or knee.

hippocampus: a small area of the brain in the temporal lobe that is responsible for emotion and memory.

hormone: a chemical released into the bloodstream by an endocrine gland or organ.

humerus: the upper arm bone.

hypertrophy: the enlargement of an organ or tissue from the increase in size of its cells.

hypothalamus: a small organ at the base of the brain where the nervous and endocrine systems interact.

hypothermia: a dangerous drop in body temperature, usually caused by prolonged exposure to extremely cold temperatures.

immune system: the network of cells in your body that fight invading cells.

inertia: the resistance of an object to a change in its motion.

infection: the invasion and multiplication of microorganisms such as bacteria, viruses, and parasites that are not normally present within the body.

inflammation: when part of the body becomes reddened, swollen, hot, and often painful, especially as a reaction to injury or infection.

inhibitory: something that slows or stops neurons from firing.

insertion point: the place where one end of a skeletal muscle is attached to a bone that moves when the muscle contracts.

insulin: a hormone produced in the pancreas that regulates the amount of glucose in the blood.

interact: how things act when they are together.

intercostal: a muscle located between the ribs.

interneurons: neurons that communicate between sensory and motor neurons.

inversely: when something increases in relation to a decrease in another thing or vice versa.

involuntary muscle: a smooth muscle that contracts without a person thinking about it.

ion: a particle with either a positive or negative charge.

irritability: the ability of a muscle to respond to stimulation.

joint: the point where two bones meet and move relative to one another.

kinesiology: the science of human movement.

kinetic energy: the work an object can perform due to its motion.

kinetics: the study of the impact that different forces have on mechanical systems, such as your body.

Krebs cycle: a series of chemical reactions in the cell's mitochondria by which most living cells generate energy in one part of the process of aerobic respiration.

lactic acid: an acid produced in the muscle cells and red blood cells when the body breaks down carbohydrates to use for energy and oxygen levels are low.

lever: a strong bar that is used to lift and move something heavy.

ligament: a tissue that connects and holds bones together.

linear motion: movement in a straight line.

liver: an organ that cleans the blood and has an important role in digestion.

load: the opposing force to be moved in a lever system.

long bone: bones that are longer than they are wide and function to support body weight and facilitate movement.

longitudinal: lengthwise.

lumen: the inside space of a tube-like structure, such as an artery.

lungs: a pair of organs located within the chest that remove carbon dioxide from and bring oxygen to the blood and are part of the respiratory system.

macro-trauma: a large injury that results from a single blow or event, such as a broken bone or dislocated joint.

mass: a measure of the amount of matter in an object.

matter: anything that has weight and takes up space.

mechanical load: the effect of a force on the body.

membrane: a thin covering.

mental health: a person's emotional and psychological well-being.

metabolism: a set of chemical reactions within the cells of living things that allow them to grow, reproduce, maintain their structure, and respond to the environment.

micro-trauma: also known as an overuse injury, it includes small rips or tears in the cartilage, ligaments, or tendons that cause discomfort and can get worse over time.

mineral: a substance found in nature that is not an animal or a plant.

mineralization: a biological process in which organic substances are converted to inorganic substances.

mitochondria: an organelle in the cell where the processes of respiration and energy production take place.

molecule: a unit of matter consisting of two or more atoms.

motion: a change in position over a unit of time.

motor neurons: the neurons that activate muscle fibers.

motor system: the organs and systems involved in movement.

motor unit: a motor neuron and the muscle fibers that it activates.

muscle: a tissue that contains cells called fibers that contract and can convert chemical energy into mechanical energy.

muscle force: the force exerted by a muscle.

muscle spindle: a sensory receptor located in the muscle that detects changes in muscle length.

muscle unit: all the muscle fibers connected to the same motor neuron.

myofibril: a cylinder of muscle protein made up of stacked sarcomeres. Myofibrils are the units of a muscle fiber.

myofilaments: the thick and thin filaments of a muscle fiber.

myosin: the protein in the thick filament of a muscle fiber.

nerve impulse: a signal transmitted along a nerve fiber.

nerves: fibers that transmit messages from the brain to the body and vice versa.

nervous system: the communication system of the body, made of nerve cells that connect the brain and extend through the body.

neurological: relating to the brain and the nervous system.

neuromuscular: relating to the nervous system and the voluntary muscles.

neuron: a single nerve cell.

neurotransmitter: a brain chemical that carries information throughout the brain and body.

nicotinamide adenine dinucleotide hydride (NADH): an electron carrier in the electron transport chain stage of aerobic respiration.

node: a connection point.

noradrenaline: a neurotransmitter that is secreted in response to stress.

nucleus: the part of the cell that controls how it functions.

nutrients: the substances in food that living things need to live and grow.

obese: excessively overweight.

organelles: structures within a cell that have a special function.

organs: a part of an organism that is self-contained and has a specific vital function, such as the heart or liver in humans.

origin point: the place where one end of a voluntary muscle is attached to a bone that remains relatively fixed.

ossification: the process of forming and hardening new bone tissue.

osteoblast: an osteocyte that forms new bone.

osteoclast: an osteocyte that dissolves and resorbs old bone.

osteocytes: bone cells that are involved in growing and shaping new bone.

oxygen: a chemical element with the symbol O.

oxygenated: filled with oxygen.

parasympathetic nervous system: one part of the autonomic nervous system that decreases heart rate.

parathyroid gland: a gland that regulates calcium, located behind the thyroid gland in the neck.

perimysium: the protective sheath covering bundles of muscle fibers called fascicles.

peripheral: something on the edge.

peripheral nervous system: the system of nerves that spreads through the body.

pH: a measure of whether something is acidic or basic.

phosphate: inorganic compounds containing the element phosphorous.

phosphocreatine: a molecule that can supply a quick burst of energy to muscles.

phosphorus: a chemical element with symbol P and atomic number 15.

physicist: a scientist who studies physical forces, including matter, energy, and motion, and how these forces interact with each other.

physics: the study of physical forces, including matter, energy, and motion, and how these forces interact with each other.

pineal: a small, cone-shaped endocrine organ that secretes melatonin.

pituitary gland: a major gland in the endocrine system that produces hormones that control other glands and many body functions, including growth.

pivot joint: a type of joint that allows side-to-side movement, such as the joint at the top of the spine that allows the head to pivot.

plasma: the colorless fluid part of blood.

plateau: a state of little or no change following a period of activity or progress.

platelets: blood cells that help the blood clot, which helps stop a cut from bleeding.

porosity: the quality of being porous, or full of tiny holes.

posterior: the back of something.

posture: the position of your body when you stand, walk, or sit.

primary source: an artifact, document, diary, manuscript, autobiography, recording, or other source of information that was created during a particular time period.

propel: to drive or move forward.

properties: characteristics, qualities, or distinctive features of something.

proprioception: an awareness of the position of the body.

proprioceptor: a sensory receptor that receives stimuli from within the body about position and movement.

protein: nutrient that is essential to the growth and repair of tissue.

protrusions: something that sticks out.

pyruvate: a molecule produced by the process of anaerobic glycolysis, which is converted into lactic acid in the muscles. Also called pyruvic acid.

reaction time: the time it takes to respond to a stimulus.

receptors: structures that receive stimuli and produce a nerve impulse to send the information.

rectilinear: made with or having straight lines.

red blood cells: blood cells that contain hemoglobin, which allows them to carry oxygen and carbon dioxide through the bloodstream.

reflex: an involuntary and often instantaneous movement in response to a stimulus.

remodeling: a process where mature bone tissue is removed from the skeleton and new bone tissue is formed.

resistance: an opposing or slowing force.

resorption: the process of breaking down and absorbing old bone.

respiration: the act of breathing, a process in living organisms that involves the production of energy, typically with the intake of oxygen and the release of carbon dioxide.

respiratory system: a system of organs that take in oxygen and expel carbon dioxide from the body. The lungs are the primary organ of the respiratory system.

reticulum: a network of tubular membranes within the cytoplasm of the cell.

RICE: an abbreviation for the treatment of soft tissue injuries: Rest, Ice, Compression, and Elevation.

rotation: the action of rotating around an axis or center.

sacrum: a triangular bone in the lower back that is located between the two hipbones of the pelvis.

sarcomere: a segment of contracting tissue that stacks to make up the myofibrils that, in turn, make up the muscle.

sarcoplasmic reticulum: a membrane system in a muscle fiber that stores and releases calcium to trigger a muscle contraction.

scaffolding: a structure used to support something.

sedentary: inactive and spending a lot of time sitting.

sensory neurons: nerve cells within the nervous system that convert external stimuli from the environment into internal electrical impulses.

serotonin: a neurotransmitter that is believed to affect mood.

sesamoid: a small bone embedded in a tendon or a muscle.

shaft: the long narrow part of an object.

shear: a force that acts parallel to a contact surface.

short bone: a small bone shaped like a cube that provides stability while still allowing for movement.

simple machine: a mechanical device that changes the direction or magnitude of a force.

sinoatrial node: a specialized muscle tissue in the wall of the right atrium of the heart that acts as a pacemaker by producing a signal to contract at regular intervals.

skeletal muscle: muscles that are attached to bones by tendons and are responsible for all movement of the body. They are also known as voluntary muscles.

skeletal system: the entire system of bones that make up your body.

sleep apnea: a sleep disorder in which breathing repeatedly stops and starts.

smooth muscle: an involuntary muscle that cannot be consciously controlled. Smooth muscle often lines the body's organs.

spinal cord: the body's major nerve cells that connect the brain to the rest of the body.

spindles: sensory fibers in muscle that work to prevent overstretching.

stability: being steady and well balanced.

static electricity: an electric charge usually produced by friction between two objects.

stimulate: to encourage action.

strength training: a type of physical exercise that uses resistance to cause muscle contractions that build the strength, size, and anaerobic endurance of skeletal muscles.

strenuous: requiring great exertion.

stress fracture: tiny cracks in bone, often caused by overuse.

stretch reflex: the automatic response of a muscle to a sudden and unexpected increase in length.

striated: having a striped appearance.

stroke: a lack of oxygen to part of the brain caused by the blocking or breaking of a blood vessel.

sympathetic nervous system: a part of the autonomic nervous system that increases heart rate.

synapse: a small gap between two nerve cells through which an electrical impulse carrying information travels.

synergist: a muscle that works together with another muscle to make movement.

synovial joint: a joint that has a space between two bones that is filled with cushioning synovial fluid.

T cell: a type of white blood cell.

technology: tools, methods, and systems used to solve a problem or do work.

tendon: a tissue that connects muscles to bones.

tension: a pulling force.

terminal: the end of something.

thymus: a gland that produces T cells for the immune system.

thyroid: a large gland in the neck that secretes hormones regulating growth and development through the rate of metabolism.

tissue: a large mass of similar cells that make up a part of an organism and perform a specific function.

torsion: a twisting force.

torso: the human body except the head, arms, and legs.

tropomyosin: a protein involved in regulating the interaction between actin and myosin in muscle contraction.

troponin: a molecule that is part of the thin filament in a muscle fiber.

trunk: see torso.

twisting: the action of turning or rotating on an axis.

twitch: a description of the speed and frequency of a nerve signal to the muscle.

valve: a structure that controls the passage of fluid through a tube.

vein: a blood vessel that carries blood back to the heart.

ventricle: one of the two lower chambers of the heart that pump blood out of the heart.

venules: very small veins.

vertebrae: the small bones that form the backbone.

virus: a submicroscopic agent that infects living organisms, often causing disease.

visual: relating to sight or seeing.

voluntary muscle: a muscle that a person controls by thinking about movement.

white blood cells: blood cells that are part of the body's immune system. They protect against infection by destroying diseased cells and germs.

Z-line: a structure that connects two sarcomeres.

METRIC CONVERSIONS

Use this chart to find the metric equivalents to the English measurements in an activity. If you need to know a half measurement, divide by two. If you need to know twice the measurement, multiply by two.

ENGLISH	METRIC
1 inch	2.5 centimeters
1 foot	30.5 centimeters
1 yard	0.9 meter
1 mile	1.6 kilometers
1 pound	0.5 kilogram
1 teaspoon	5 milliliters
1 tablespoon	15 milliliters
1 cup	237 milliliters

RESOURCES

BOOKS

The Body: A Complete User's Guide (Revised Edition) by Patricia Daniels, National Geographic, 2014.

Body: The Complete Human by Patricia S. Daniels, Lisa Stein, and Trisha Gura, National Geographic, 2009.

Ultimate Bodypedia: An Amazing Inside-Out Tour of the Human Body by Patricia Daniels, Christina Wilsdon, and Jen Agresta, National Geographic, 2014.

How the Body Works, DK Publishing, 2016.

The Concise Book of Muscles by Chris Jarmey and John Sharkey, North Atlantic Books, 2016.

Anatomy Explained by Abigail King, Rosen, 2015.

The Everything Guide to Anatomy and Physiology: All You Need to Know About How the Human Body Works by Kevin Langford, Adams Media, 2015.

How Cells Send, Receive, and Process Information by Marc Mclaughlin, Michael Friedman, and Brett Friedman, Rosen Educational Service, 2015.

WEBSITES

healthline.com/human-body-maps
This Healthline site uses detailed 3-D models of body parts—including muscles, veins, bones, and organs—to understand how the human body works.

getbodysmart.com
This site uses animated text narrations and quizzes to explore human body systems, including the skeletal system, muscular system, circulatory system, and more.

innerbody.com
This site offers hundreds of interactive anatomy pictures and descriptions of the various body systems, including the skeletal system, muscular system, and nervous system.

kidshealth.org/en/kids/muscles.html
Learn more about the body's muscles at this site.

biology4kids.com/files/systems_main.html
Visit this website for basic information about a variety of biology and human body topics.

QR CODE GLOSSARY

Page 20:
innerbody.com/image/skelfov.html

Page 23:
innerbody.com/image_skelfov/skel20_new.html

Page 32:
youtube.com/watch?v=1A2LUbJjDQ0

Page 34:
innerbody.com

Page 34:
realbodywork.com/articles/anatomy-games/

Page 40:
innerbody.com/image_skel13/ligm27.html

Page 41:
innerbody.com/image/musfov.html

Page 48:
youtube.com/watch?v=nvXuq9jRWKE

Page 49:
koshland-science-museum.org/explore-the-science/interactives/brain-anatomy

Page 62:
pbslearningmedia.org/resource/tdc02.sci.life.stru.circulator/from-the-heart

Page 85:
youtube.com/watch?v=Ak17BWJ3bLg

INDEX

A

abduction and adduction, 31
acceleration, law of, 4
actin filaments, 27, 32–34, 99
action and reaction, law of, 4
action potential, 39, 47
activities (Inquire & Investigate)
 Breathe In, Breathe Out, 76
 Build a Model of the Arm, 23
 Build a Working Hand Model, 40
 The Effect of Exercise
  on the Brain, 105
 The Effect of Exercise on
  Lung Capacity, 106–107
 The Endocrine System:
  Fight or Flight?, 74–75
 Extracting Energy From
  Sugar, 88–89
 Finding Levers in the Body, 42
 Hormones: The Body's
  Communicators, 73
 How Much Chemical Energy
  Is In Your Food?, 90–91
 Involuntary Reflex, 56–57
 Not Enough Fuel: Muscle
  Fatigue, 87
 Test Your Reaction Speed, 55
 What Makes Bones Strong?, 24
 Working in Pairs, 41
adenosine triphosphate (ATP), 78–87
adrenals, 70, 72
aerobic respiration, 80, 84–86
amyotrophic lateral
 sclerosis (ALS), 50
anaerobic glycolysis, 80, 81–83
angular motion, 7
Archimedes, vi
Aristotle, vi, 6
arteries, 62–63. See also blood
 and blood vessels
athletics, vi, 6, 7, 68, 78, 81.
 See also exercise

B

balance, 52–53
basal ganglia, 49
bending, 5
biomechanics, vii, 6–7
blood and blood vessels, vi,
 9–10, 12, 15, 16, 28, 61–64,
 67–70, 72, 95–96
bones. See skeletal system
brain-body connection, 8, 43–57
 balance via, 52–53
 brain structure and role in, 48–49
 exercise vs. inactivity affecting,
  10, 95, 96, 99–102, 105
 muscular system messages
  from, 27–28, 32, 33, 35, 39,
  44, 47, 48, 50–51, 52–54
 nervous system in, 8, 27–28,
  32, 33, 45–46, 47, 48,
  54, 69, 71, 95, 96, 99
 reflexes via, 47, 53–54, 56–57, 99
 sending signals via, 46–47, 48
 senses in, 51–54
bursa, 19

C

calcium, 13, 14, 15, 24, 33, 35
cancellous bone, 15
capillaries, 63
cardiovascular system, 9–10, 28,
 60–66, 69–70, 72, 95. See
 also blood and blood vessels
cartilage, 12–13, 18–19, 20
cerebellum, 49
cerebral cortex, 48, 50
circulatory system. See
 cardiovascular system
compression loads, 5, 97
connective tissue, 19–21, 32. See
 also ligaments; tendons
cortical bone, 14–15

D

da Vinci, Leonardo, vii
dementia, 96, 100, 105
dendrites, 46–47
digestive system, 27–28,
 69–70, 79, 96
double jointedness, 18

E

elasticity, 36
electron transport chain, 85, 86
endocrine system, 60, 70–75, 96, 104
endurance, 34–35
energy, fuel for. See fuel
exercise, 9–10, 93–107.
 See also athletics
 benefits of, 9–10, 94
 blood flow during, 69–70
 brain/mind affected by, 10,
  95, 96, 99–102, 105
 excessive or too much, 102–104
 fuel for and after, 78, 81, 100
 heart rate during, 64–66
 inactivity vs., 9–10, 94–96
 mental health affected by,
  10, 96, 101–102
 muscular system affected by,
  9, 94–96, 97–99, 100
 skeletal system affected by,
  9–10, 22, 94–95, 97
extension, 31, 36

F

fascicles, 28
fight-or-flight response, 74–75
flavin adenine dinucleotide
 hydride (FADH2), 85, 86
flexibility, 18, 19
flexion, 31
forces and motion, 1–10, 22, 34–39,
 53–54, 63–64, 97, 98–99

fuel, 77–91
  adenosine triphosphate as, 78–87
  aerobic respiration for, 80, 84–86
  anaerobic glycolysis
    for, 80, 81–83
  exercise and, 78, 81, 100
  hormones and, 71–72
  oxygen as, 66–68, 69, 76.
    See also oxygen
  phosphocreatine for, 80, 81

G

Galen, vi
Galilei, Galileo, vii
Galvani, Luigi, vii
general motion, 7
glucose and glycogen, 72, 79, 82–86
Golgi tendon organ, 52, 53, 54, 99
gravity, 4, 5, 64, 97
Gulick, Luther Halsey, vii

H

Harvey, William, vii
heart, 9–10, 28, 60–62, 64–66, 95.
  See also cardiovascular system
hemoglobin, 67–68, 69
Herodicus, vi
Hippocrates, vi
hormones, 70–74, 96, 104
human movement
  brain-body connection for, 8, 10,
    27–28, 32, 33, 35, 39, 43–57,
    69, 71, 95, 96, 99–102, 105
  exercise and, 9–10, 22, 64–66,
    69–70, 78, 81, 93–107.
    See also athletics
  forces and motion for,
    1–10, 22, 34–39, 53–54,
    63–64, 97, 98–99
  fuel for, 66–68, 69, 71–72,
    76, 77–91, 100

key questions on, 10, 22,
    39, 54, 72, 86, 104
  kinesiology as study of, vi, 3, 6
  laws of motion for, vii, 3–4
  muscular system and, 8,
    9, 25–42, 44, 47, 48,
    50–51, 52–54, 60–70,
    79–87, 94–96, 97–99, 100
  organs and organ systems'
    role in, 9–10, 27–28, 59–76,
    79, 95–96, 104, 106–107
  skeletal system and, 8, 9–10, 11–
    24, 27, 29, 37, 64, 94–95, 97
  timeline of, vi–vii
hypothalamus, 70

I

immune system, 10, 96
inertia, law of, 4
irritability, 36

J

joint capsules, 20
joints, 18–19, 21–22, 37

K

key questions, 10, 22, 39,
    54, 72, 86, 104
kinesiology, vi, 3, 6
Krebs cycle, 85–86

L

lactic acid, 83, 84
laws of motion, vii, 3–4
lever systems, 37–39, 42
ligaments, 17, 18, 19, 20–21, 22
linear motion, 6–7
loads, 5–6, 37–39, 97, 98–99
lungs, 60, 61, 66–69, 76, 106–107

M

Marey, Étienne-Jules, vii
mental health, 10, 96, 101–102
metabolism, 80
motion. *See also* human movement
  forms of, 6–7
  laws of, vii, 3–4
  range of, 21
motor neuron diseases, 50
muscular dystrophy, 36
muscular system, 8, 25–42
  artificial muscles simulating, 32
  brain-nervous system messages
    to, 27–28, 32, 33, 35, 39,
    44, 47, 48, 50–51, 52–54
  cardiovascular muscles in,
    28, 60–66, 69. *See also*
    cardiovascular system
  for endurance, 34–35
  exercise vs. inactivity affecting,
    9, 94–96, 97–99, 100
  fast, slow and intermediate
    fibers in, 34–35
  for force, 34–39, 53–54
  fuel for, 79–87, 100
  lever systems with, 37–39, 42
  muscle composition in, 28–29, 32
  muscle contraction in, 27–29,
    30, 32–34, 35, 36, 53–54, 64
  muscle properties in, 36
  muscle spindles in, 52, 53, 54
  muscle types in, 27–28
  number of muscles in, 26
  pairs of muscles in, 29–31, 41
  proprioceptors in, 52–53
  respiratory muscles in, 66–70.
    See also respiratory system
  stretching muscles in, 53–54
  synergists in, 31
myofibrils, 32, 34
myosin filaments, 27, 32–34, 99

INDEX

N

nervous system, 8, 27–28, 32, 33, 45–46, 47, 48, 54, 69, 71, 95, 96, 99. *See also* brain-body connection
neurons, 46–47, 49, 50–52
neurotransmitters, 47
Newton's laws of motion, vii, 3–4
nicotinamide adenine dinucleotide hydride (NADH), 85, 86

O

organs and organ systems, 59–76
    cardiovascular system, 9–10, 28, 60–66, 69–70, 72, 95. *See also* blood and blood vessels
    digestive system, 27–28, 69–70, 79, 96
    endocrine system, 60, 70–75, 96, 104
    exercise *vs.* inactivity affecting, 9–10, 95–96, 106–107
    immune system, 10, 96
    respiratory system, 60, 61, 66–70, 76, 106–107
    smooth muscles in, 27–28
osteocytes, 13
oxygen, 12, 16, 60, 61, 62, 63, 64, 65, 66–69, 76, 84, 95

P

pancreas, 72
parathyroid, 71
phosphocreatine, 80, 81
physical activity. *See* athletics; exercise
pineal body, 70
pituitary, 70, 72
proprioceptors, 52–53

R

range of motion, 21
reflexes, 47, 53–54, 56–57, 99
respiratory system, 60, 61, 66–70, 76, 106–107

S

sarcomeres, 27, 32, 34
senses, 51–54
shear loads, 5, 6
skeletal muscles, 27, 29, 37, 64
skeletal system, 8, 11–24
    appendicular skeleton in, 13, 16
    axial skeleton in, 13, 16
    bone composition in, 14–15
    bone development for, 12–13, 14, 22
    bone marrow in, 15, 16
    bone types in, 16–17
    connective tissue for, 19–21. *See also* ligaments; tendons
    exercise vs. inactivity affecting, 9–10, 22, 94–95, 97
    joints in, 18–19, 21–22, 37
    number of bones in, 20
    skeletal muscles attaching to, 27, 29, 37, 64
smoking, 76
smooth muscles, 27–28
sports. *See* athletics; exercise
sugar, 72, 79, 82, 88–89, 96. *See also* glucose and glycogen
synapses, 46–47
synergists, 31

T

tendons, 17, 20–21, 22, 29. *See also* Golgi tendon organ
tension, 5, 36, 54
thyroid, 70
timeline, vi–vii
torsion, 5, 6

V

veins, 63–64. *See also* blood and blood vessels

Z

Z line, 32